www.constablerobinson.com/rightway

SUCCESSFUL PROPERTY LETTING

HOW TO MAKE MONEY IN BUY-TO-LET

David Lawrenson

RIGHT WAY

Constable & Robinson Ltd
3 The Lanchesters
162 Fulham Palace Road
London W6 9ER
www.constablerobinson.com

First published in the UK 2005

This new completely revised and updated edition
published by Right Way, an imprint of
Constable & Robinson, 2011

A copy of the British Library Cataloguing in Publication
Data is available from the British Library

ISBN: 978-0-7160-2275-6

Printed and bound in the EU

1 3 5 7 9 10 8 6 4 2

DEDICATION

To Dagmar Svehlik, my partner, for her fantastic love and support, and to Alex, our son.

ABOUT THE AUTHOR

After university and his MBA at Cass (formerly City University) Business School, David Lawrenson worked in the financial services industry as an internal consultant and project manager.

In 2002, he left to become a full-time property investor. Then in 2005, the first edition of *Successful Property Letting – How to Make Money in Buy-to-Let* came out and became the UK's top-selling property book.

Lawrenson is now in constant demand as a writer and media commentator on buy-to-let issues. He is quoted regularly in national newspapers like *The Times, Independent* and *Daily Telegraph* and he writes for many property magazines and buy-to-let websites. He is a regular speaker at trade shows and for public and private organisations and trade associations and runs a thriving consultancy business which helps banks, building societies, investment funds, letting agents, local authorities and housing associations with their products and services for the buy-to-let and landlord markets.

Lawrenson also has a low-cost seminar programme and a one-to-one consultancy service for people wishing to get into buy-to-let for the first time as well as for more experienced investors. His website and blog are at *www.LettingFocus.com* and David can be contacted at *david@LettingFocus.com*.

CONTENTS

1

AN INTRODUCTION TO PROPERTY INVESTMENT

Why you need this book
This book is about how to make a success of property investment through letting residential property. I will tell you what you *really* need to know to make money in the buy-to-let market and talk you right through the residential letting business.

This book will be of interest to people who are thinking of becoming landlords for the first time as well as those with more experience. It will tell you where to buy, what to buy, how to spot locations that are on the up, how to buy at auction, below market value and "off plan", how to arrange finance, how to find good tenants and how to look after them.

If you need to do work on your property, it will tell you how to hire builders and architects, how to deal with planning and building regulations and how to furnish and decorate your property.

You'll also learn all you need to know about your legal responsibilities as a landlord, what to do if things go wrong, how to minimise tax on your rental profits and how to buy abroad.

When you've read this book you'll know how to let out property successfully, either by yourself or with the help of an agent whilst keeping your costs and time to a minimum. You'll know what the big risks are, what sort of things to look out for and how to avoid disasters. You'll know how to keep your tenants happy and the rent rolling in!

This book is kept regularly updated to reflect the current conditions in the property market.

A brief history of residential property letting

You've probably heard about people who have made a fortune out of property investment and about a few people who have lost money too. The subject comes up at a lot of dinner parties. And the news is full of it too.

These days, there is always some survey or other on how house prices are moving, how long it's taking to sell properties, how rents are doing or what the ratio of this to that or the other is. In the British Isles we seem to be obsessed about it. And now that some of us are busy buying up properties abroad, we'll no doubt have to worry about house price to earnings ratios in Croatia and Barbados too! However, property hasn't always been the obsession it is today.

In the old days, people lived with their parents for a long time and moved only when (or after) they got married. The proportion of people who owned their own home was much less than it is today. People tended to rent and if they bought property at all it was at a later stage in life and only after years spent building up a savings account at the local building society.

Mortgage loans were hard to obtain and small, relative

to the value of the properties they financed. The "flexible" labour market, where employers could make people redundant because their companies weren't making *enough* profit hadn't yet been invented.

In the housing shortage after the Second World War, a few nasty landlords emerged who overcharged and used intimidation tactics against their tenants. One landlord, a certain Mr Rachman, led to the word "Rachmanism" becoming forever associated with particularly unpleasant landlord practices.

In response, the Government typically overreacted and passed laws that set up what were called Rent Act tenancies. These gave tenants a protected low rent but it became difficult if not impossible for landlords to get their property back. Faced with low returns and little flexibility huge numbers of landlords simply withdrew from the market, resulting in the proportion of properties in the private rented sector falling from 50 per cent in 1945 to less than 10 per cent by the mid 1980s and a shortage of homes to let. Ultimately, this started to harm the economy because people found they couldn't move to jobs in other areas because there were so few homes available to rent.

Finally the Government saw sense and in 1988 and 1996 passed the Housing Acts which made it much easier and quicker for landlords to reclaim possession of their property at the end of a letting. The buy-to-let mortgage followed and the proportion of UK housing stock that is privately rented is now near to 15 per cent (and much higher in some urban areas.)

"Landlord" or "Property Investor"

The word "landlord" has some negative connotations and I suppose this goes back to the medieval times of Lords and

Serfs but it was made worse by the activities of Rachman. There are a few rogue landlords still out there today. One in particular is especially notorious, but as he seems to spend fortunes suing people, I won't give my publisher (or myself) any sleepless nights by naming him. In general, though, successful landlords these days are ones who look after their tenants and treat them with respect. As a result, the negative associations of the word "landlord" are dying away too, so I'll stick with it throughout this book.

How property differs from other types of investment

With property, unlike many other kinds of investments, you're the one in control, not some anonymous fund manager in the city. You can walk past your property and actually see your investment so you are immediately more connected to it. I wouldn't go around hugging the walls of your property while the tenants are there, but I'm sure you understand what I mean when I say you can start to love property!

Property also provides something we all need – shelter so there should always be demand for it. With property, you can sell it whenever you want, which you can't do with a pension. Unlike a pension, you can also bequeath it to your heirs when you die.

At this point I'll admit to being cannier at investing in property than I am in the stock market. More than once I've bought a share, only to see the price collapse. I find this somewhat baffling because surely, if the Report and Accounts of a company have been read by a good many clever people (including highly paid fund managers) and the company shares are, say, one pound, then how they can fall to a penny over the course of just one year (or even less time) is a mystery. Maybe the Report and Accounts are meaningless!

Of course, in the stock market, the risk is that the products or services of a company can go out of fashion, be replaced by new technology or simply end up being managed by people who lose all the company's money and then get a big payoff for doing so!

The problems don't stop with individual shares either. The audit and regulatory bodies have clearly failed to protect people from endowment and pension mis-selling. Add to this, the split capital trusts scandal and low returns on shares in general and it's easy to see why property is now seen as a good way of providing a reliable secondary income or a retirement fund.

The fact is that with property, if you do your homework and check out the location and the local tenant market, you'll know a lot more than you can ever learn about any company in any published source.

If you combine letting property with a day job, you'll have the satisfaction of knowing that if your boss suddenly decides your face no longer fits you'll still have the income and capital from your property to fall back on. This can give a great sense of security.

If you're a full-time landlord, you'll have an income stream that's reliable and you can choose how and when you work. Want a lie in? Then have one. You're the boss!

Now that everyone and his dog are talking about property it's easy to imagine that the market is being swamped with too many developers and too many properties to rent. And as salary to mortgage multiples becomes more stretched, the fear is that house price rises may level out or fall a bit.

However, if we step back and look at the big picture,

we can see that an increasing population and a shortage of houses, including "social housing" are forcing prices up. The growing population is driven not so much by internal growth but by immigration. Also, divorce means that some people are tending to live in smaller units with the number of one-person homes set to continue to grow markedly. At the same time there has been a recent big increase in the number of families who rent from private landlords. Housing supply has failed to keep up with these changes and demand for housing, especially in London and the South-East, is outstripping supply.

It is clear that the UK needs a massive house-building programme to close the gap. The hopes of the Government to meet housing demand by streamlining the planning system have worked only partially and in recent years tough credit conditions have made it hard for builders to get funds to build and borrowers to get mortgages.

So, a continued lack of housing seems to suggest that a big fall in property prices like the one between 1989 and 1994 is unlikely – and whilst first-time buyers are clearly more stretched today, houses are still affordable in many areas, especially for those lucky first-time buyers able to rely on help from their parents.

In the rental market the trends to more job flexibility, temporary workers, more students, more migrant workers, less council/social housing and increasing divorce rates are all factors that should lead to increasing demand for rental accommodation. If there is no signifi-cant growth in the number of houses built, then the outlook for rents should be up too.

Changes in government tax policy may also boost property. To encourage more rented housing, the

Government has bought in a new form of tax efficient property fund based on so called "real estate investment trusts" or "REITS" which have proved popular in other countries.

And with a diminishing stock of council housing the Government is paying an increasingly hefty housing benefit bill – a lot of which ends up with private landlords.

When to buy? Good and bad times in the property market

There are undoubtedly some times that are better than others in the property market. However, even in bad times there are still opportunities for the experienced property investor. Let's take a look at a time that is probably regarded as pretty dire: in spring 1989, house prices peaked over most of the UK and started a decline that went on until 1994.

Nevertheless, even then, there were certain areas and certain types of property that didn't fall in value too much. This was usually due to local factors – a new road, tube, railway, airport or employment opportunities. Rents actually went up over the period 1989 to 1994, so if you got the right property in the right place, this was still a good time to invest.

The skill of the property investor and landlord is in identifying these local opportunities and acting on them. To do this you need local knowledge and I shall say more about how to do this in Chapter 3. Property does indeed have risks but, if you do your homework, these risks are manageable. To some extent risks with property are reduced because the market has a natural compensating mechanism in which any weakness in house prices is counterbalanced by strength in rents. Let me explain.

When house prices fall, as they did in 2008 and 2009 due to the effects of a tightening of mortgage availability, first-time buyers tend to stay on the sidelines and rent, hoping to buy at cheaper prices later. This tends to push up rents. At the same time, nervousness among some home-owners and inexperienced landlords (and harsh credit conditions) may lead them to sell their properties and rent instead. This can have the effect of reducing the number of properties available to rent at the same time as further increasing demand for rented accommodation. The higher demand for rentals pushes up rents and compensates for falls in house prices. Indeed, this was the picture in the UK between 1989 and 1994, a period of generally falling house prices but rising rents.

Conversely, when house prices rise and look set to rise further, first-time buyers (who might otherwise have rented but are fearful of missing the boat) enter the market to buy property and the opposite effect happens. With less demand for rented accommodation, rents may tend to be static or fall but the price of property should go up. This was the picture in the late 1990s and into the start of the new millennium.

Meet the people who want your money

As interest in property as an investment has grown, so too has the number of players involved in the business. There are mortgage lenders, mortgage brokers, surveyors, solicitors, letting agents, freeholders, managing agents, developers, property syndicates, buying agents, consultants, and last, but not least, the taxman. The thing they have in common is: they all want your money!

There are even people who give seminars on letting property, where they aim to teach you all you need to know in a weekend in exchange for a few hundred (or even thousand) pounds and the opportunity to join their investment club, where you're supposed to be able to get big discounts off new developments. Then there are buying agents who'll purchase and kit out investment property for you.

The standard of performance and value for money of many of these players is variable (and some are little better than cowboys) and I'll comment further on each of them throughout the book. I'll also tell you how to get the best out of them, where you can find good advisers and how you can minimise the amount of money that you pay them.

For now it is worth your being aware that most aspects of residential property investment advice are not regulated which makes property a very attractive area of business to the charlatan looking to separate naïve investors from their savings. You have been warned.

Is it for you?
What kind of person makes a successful landlord?
The sort of person who makes a good landlord is someone who is sceptical and enquiring and has good people and communication skills. They are usually good administrators and, above all, they really love the property business and are prepared to take some risks.

Successful landlords question everything they hear and are prepared to do their own research. So if a developer or a consultant at a seminar tells them that his new development of 10,000 identikit flats in Liverpool is going to be a fantastic investment, they don't take this at face value.

If a director of a big bank says the housing market is going to grow rapidly, then be aware he has a vested interest in saying this, i.e. to sell more mortgages. Just because he is Chief Executive of an FTSE 100 company and earns more in a week than you make in a year doesn't mean you should listen to him. Similarly, if an investment bank says house prices will collapse, ask yourself could they just be saying that in order to persuade people to invest in stock market based funds instead?

Be sceptical of what you learn at consultants' seminars. Most people say they learned nothing that they couldn't learn from reading a book. Generally they just got a hard sell to invest in new developments, the idea being that the syndicate used investors' money to win supposedly big discounts on new-build properties, source non-existent "below market value" stock or buy "soon to-be-refurbed" properties on "no go" estates. Probably the biggest losers are the many novice investors who bought off-plan new-build flats on big developments from syndicates mainly, though not entirely in inner cities in the English North and Midlands, who have seen the values of their properties collapse and the flats hard to let out.

So beware. You can do well in property but it's simply not the case that you can make a million in a year without taking what to most people are unacceptably large risks. People who say you can do this are talking nonsense.

A lot of new-build off-plan schemes these days are for developments abroad. The consultant or developer may even pay the cost of the airfare and transport to the development and use high-pressure selling techniques with lots of free drink to get otherwise intelligent people to part with their money.

The hard fact is that you must be prepared to do some work. Not a lot of work, but some work nevertheless! Listen to what people say, but do your own research too before committing to anything. Keep in mind that currently there is no protection under the Financial Services Act for people who invest in property or via property syndicates. So be careful.

It helps to be good with people as you'll need to form good relationships with your tenants and anyone who does work for you. I don't mean that you should be their best mate. Far from it! But you must be professional and courteous as well as firm and fair.

When dealing with tenants, there is no point being mean and arguing over small things or small amounts of money. As in life, if you treat tenants with respect they'll repay you in kind. The same applies for tradesmen. Pay them promptly because, if you don't, you can't expect them to rush out when you really need them.

It's important to be a clear communicator. Prospective tenants must know exactly what they're getting with the property they'll be renting. They must understand when the contract starts and what their responsibilities are under the tenancy agreement. If you use letting agents, they should understand what you expect of them too. The same applies to builders and decorators. You cannot be too clear!

It helps to be organised and have a good filing system to keep track of income, costs and repairs. Things should be fixed quickly and phone calls returned as soon as possible. You don't need to do the actual work yourself or be particularly practical. I'm not, but I know just enough

Case study

In 2003, more than one thousand people suffered massive losses after being duped by a property investment company promising 'guaranteed' annual returns of 15 per cent. The investors, who included accountants, lawyers and doctors, handed over five and six figure sums after being seduced by the company's brochures. The firm used adverts in publications such as the *Financial Times* to tell investors they could make a fortune buying cheap properties in the north of England, which the company would refurbish and let out to 'social housing' tenants. The company would supervise all the refurbishment, find the tenants and even collect the rent. Investors would sit back and wait for the money to roll in. If only life were so simple. The company pulled in more than £100 million but much of the refurbishment work was never carried out and the tenants never materialised. It turned out that investors had bought derelict, boarded-up houses which were worth far less than they had paid for them. Some were uninhabitable and worth less than £2,000. The firm was closed down by the DTI. Most of the investors were from the south-east of England and had been persuaded that the north was 'bursting with investment opportunities within the social housing sector'. Amazingly, most of the investors hadn't visited the areas or seen the properties at all. This is not a unique story – even in 2011 we continue to see property companies going bust and lots of "investors" losing their shirts.

to avoid getting ripped off by tradesmen.

Finally, you must like property. So, if houses bore you stiff, you're probably better off doing something else. I freely admit to being an addict and, like any successful landlord, I find it impossible to walk past an estate agency without looking in the window at house prices, rental levels, etc. You should be the same.

Follow the six commandments set out below and you'll make a success of property investment:

1. You must buy the right type of property at the right time at a good price in the right location.
2. You must do all you can to minimise vacant periods when the property isn't let.
3. You must take care vetting tenants to avoid having a bad one.
4. You must fix things promptly and cost-effectively.
5. You must be good at dealing with administration – in particular, you must keep account of all your income and costs and have a proper filing system.
6. You must be able to spot when someone isn't being straight with you.

I'll explain how to get these things right in the course of the book.

How much should I put in property?

At a recent speaking engagement I was asked, "How much should I put into property investments?"

Unless you're a highly diversified property investor in terms of the number, type and locations of properties you own, I would caution against having more than, say, 50 per cent of your money in property. However, there is no ideal percentage. How much you invest in property is whatever amount you feel comfortable with, which depends on your own attitude to risk.

It's possible to invest in the UK housing market through collective or unitised funds or through other funds that track house prices. This will give you some exposure but it won't make any real money because, if you are to have real success, you've got to get involved yourself, not give it to a fund manager who may turn out to be useless and will certainly charge a hefty fee.

Investing in property is not without risks. The biggest risk in property is a downturn in the economy. This could have the effect of making house prices and rents fall, increasing interest rates, increasing tenant default and cutting or reversing the flow of inward migration into the UK – thus reducing the pressure on housing. Another big risk is that the Government could change the way residential property investment is taxed, making it less attractive compared to other investment types.

There is also a threat from big City funds which have started to invest in the private rented sector by building huge new purpose developments exclusively for private rental – thus increasing the competition for private landlords. (Some city funds use me as a consultant in this area so I know there is genuine interest, though up to now most have kept their money in their wallets and investment has been limited so far.)

At the moment, most of your running costs, including the interest on loans to buy properties to let, are deductible against your rental income. This is, of course, one of the greatest attractions of buy-to-let as it means someone else is paying off your mortgage. The risk that the Government could change this is very low – but it is a small risk, nonetheless.

This book is about managing these and other risks and making profit at the same time. Some risk, however, will always remain – that's the price of the big rewards. If you don't like risk at all you should put this book down now and keep your money in the building society.

Any comments or suggestions on this book are appreciated. Please feel free to mail me. You can contact me by email via my website www.LettingFocus.com where I also provide buy-to-let advice and consultancy for organisations and individuals as well as writing a blog and reviewing discounted products for landlords.

Note
To avoid saying "he" and "him" instead of the clumsy phrases "he/she" and "him/her", I simply use "he"/"him" to refer to both men and women.

2

EASY AS ABC:
THE SIMPLE ECONOMICS OF
PROPERTY LETTING

Income and capital growth

How do you make money out of property investment? Well, it's quite easy. You can make it by the property going up in price (what is called capital growth) and you can make it by earning more in rent than you spend in costs (i.e. income).

Sounds simple doesn't it? The problem is that a lot of people make the mistake of overlooking **all** the costs of their investment and completely forget to account for things like running costs, the cost of their own time and the cost of using their own money. Property programmes on TV make these same mistakes too.

Many people who are new to investing in property seem to forget to budget for the cost of maintaining their investment properties at all or, if they do, they proceed in the mistaken belief that the costs of maintaining a property which is let out will cost no more than maintaining their own property. It won't!

How to calculate the true income from your property

When people talk about property, they often talk about the "property yield". And yet, this term often means different things to different people, so when you are talking about yield, even if you know what it means, it's always useful to check that the other person has the same understanding.

So, what is yield? Yield is just another way of expressing the "income" on a property relative to the value invested in it. Very simply it's just the total amount of rent, less the running costs of the property, divided by the total value invested in the property including buying costs. So if your annual rent is, say, £18,000 a year, the running costs are £2,000 per year and the total value of the property is £250,000, then the "yield" is calculated as:

Yield =

Total Rent minus Running Costs/Current Value of Property

In this case it is:

£18,000 − £2,000 running costs/£250,000 =
£16,000/£250,000 = 0.064

or, expressed as a percentage, 6.4 per cent – quite a decent yield!

Generally, it's that simple, but even with something so simple there are some potential snakes in the grass as I shall explain.

Step 1: Estimating the rent and allowing for voids
If you haven't yet bought a property, how do you work out what the rent will be? Well, you could look in the

local paper to see what rents are being charged for *equivalent* properties or you could ask a letting agent. Unfortunately, both approaches may lead you to believe you can get a higher rent than is achievable for a *permanently let property with no voids.*

I'll explain. For my properties, the rents I achieve are typically 5 to 15 per cent less than those being asked by other landlords and letting agents for the same type of property. This is not because I am a bad businessman. It's because I set my rents so my properties are always fully let whereas my competitors don't. I know this, because sometimes I pose as a tenant and go and look at other properties. (It's always good to check out the competition!) Six times out of ten, the previous tenants have left and the properties are standing empty and burning up their owners' money.

I don't doubt that sometimes other landlords and letting agents do eventually let their properties. Very often though, they'll have had to drop the rent. Even where they achieve high rents they may have been forced to agree improvements such as redecorating or buying new furniture which will hit their profit.

The period of time a property is not let, the "void period" in landlord's jargon, is extremely costly. In the example above, the annual rental was £18,000 or £1,500 per month. If the property is unlet for a month, then the annual rent falls from £18,000 to £16,500 and the effect on the yield would be to reduce it by 0.6 per cent.

In fact, the situation is worse because, with an unlet property, running costs are likely to be higher because you *may* have to pay for council tax and utilities too. Also, if the property is furnished and empty, your insurance premium could well go up as well.

You may get lucky and get a tenant to pay top dollar with no gap between tenants, so no void period at all. Your super new tenant might not even demand a new bed or cooker for his top dollar rent! But he'll probably find out soon enough he's paying a premium rent and chances are he will become more demanding and ask more of you! He may be more likely to leave after a short period and you'll have the costs of remarketing to bear.

If instead, you offer to let at a rent just below the market average, you'll have more tenant demand and be able to cherry pick the best tenants and those who can move in just after your previous tenants move out. You'll have no void period, you won't need to throw in extras to get the new tenant and you'll have someone who is happy and will stay longer because he knows he's paying a fair rent.

This isn't about being a "nice landlord". It's just good business, because those voids, additional things thrown in "free" to attract a premium rate tenant and, most of all, your time have to be paid for somehow!

Step 2: Work out your running costs
The running costs of renting out property include interest on money borrowed, letting agency fees (where a letting agent is used), ground rent and service charges (where the property is leasehold), insurance premiums, replacement of fixtures and furnishings, general maintenance including an annual gas inspection (where gas appliances are present), Energy Performance Certificates, deposit protection, advertising, legal expenses, membership of landlord organisations, phone calls, travel costs and the cost of your time. Apart from the cost of your own time, all these costs can be deducted from rental income for tax purposes.

LETTING AGENCY FEES

These are typically about one month's rent plus VAT for finding a tenant including doing reference checks, signing agreements, dealing with utilities and doing the check-in. Landlords with large portfolios may get lower charges than this though fees in London could be higher. Typically, money is deducted from the tenant's first month's rent and deposit and before any residual money is paid over to the landlord. Also, some agents "try it on" by trying to re-charge the fee each time the property is re-let to the same tenant. If the agent provides management services too, you'll need to add another 3 to 5 per cent plus VAT. Chapter 7 has some good advice on how to negotiate these costs down.

GROUND RENT AND SERVICE CHARGES

If your property is leasehold you'll have to pay ground rent and service charges. Obviously, the cost varies enormously between properties; however, it's always charged in advance. For flats, the buildings insurance premium is usually contained within the service charge.

INSURANCE PREMIUMS

Buildings insurance premiums vary depending mainly on the size of property and its location. You must have it and should budget about 3 per cent of the rent for it. Where the property is furnished, contents insurance is also a must. Allow for between 1 and 3 per cent of the rent depending on the level of furnishing. For properties with few furnishings you could opt to cover damage by having a sufficiently high deposit.

Some landlords take out separate cover against a tenant defaulting and the cost of doing this is typically 2 to 4 per cent of the rent. In addition, you can also take out insurance against things going wrong with plumbing, drains, gas, electrical appliances or whatever. I wouldn't bother with the latter for the reasons explained in Chapter 5.

REPLACEMENT FIXTURES AND FITTINGS

Build in an allowance for replacing furnishings. How much furniture you provide will depend on the type of market you're pitching at. In Chapter 5 I'll explain how to figure out, before you even buy a property, how much furnishing (if any) you need to provide. Allow for the fact that furnishings, whether white goods like washing machines or soft furnishings like sofas and beds, will wear out faster with tenants.

GENERAL MAINTENANCE

In a property which is let out, more things need maintaining more often than they do in a private home. The main things that go wrong are boilers, pipes, overflows, drains and the like. As long as young people prefer to study Media Studies rather than Plumbing, there will be a shortage of skilled plumbers and the cost of these services will continue to rise well ahead of the rate of inflation. In Chapter 8, I'll show how to keep maintenance costs in check, but you should expect costs to be 20 per cent higher than you would in a private home. Gas appliances must be checked by a registered gas engineer so you should add an additional £50 to the annual running costs for each gas appliance in the property.

ADVERTISING

If you don't use an agent, you will need to advertise for tenants. In many media you can advertise for tenants for free. However, if your property is more up-market, you may have to pay to advertise in the sort of publications or websites that your intended tenants read. Currently, you can get your property advertised on all the main portals like Right Move via landlord letting sites for about £50 or £60. See the Useful Links at LettingFocus.com

LEGAL AND OTHER REGULATORY EXPENSES

If you follow the instructions in Chapter 7 and properly reference check potential tenants, you'll be very unlucky to get a tenant who doesn't pay his rent and needs to be evicted. However, if that does happen, the good news is you won't need to employ a solicitor or lawyer. Lawyers earn quite enough money already and you can do it all on your own without having to use their services. I'll explain how to in Chapter 9. The bad news is it takes about four to six months to get rid of a really bad tenant so it's wise to budget for about half a month's rent per year to cover the cost of unpaid rent of a bad tenant, just in case.

Other regulatory type costs include an Energy Performance Certificate (once every ten years and costing about £50), tenancy deposit protection in an insured scheme (about £30), landlords' registration (Scotland only) and HMO licensing (if applicable). These are all covered later in the book.

LANDLORDS' ORGANISATIONS

For less than £100 a year, you can join a landlords' organisation and get all the news including any legal updates, helplines in case things go wrong, local meetings, access to up-to-date tenancy agreements, discounts on websites which advertise property, and money off buildings insurance, tenancy deposit schemes, energy performance certificates and building materials. Two of the biggest are the National Landlords Association and the Residential Landlords Association. (See Appendix 2 for a list of the main associations.) And check out my own blog at www.LettingFocus.com for occasional offers.

PERSONAL COSTS

Allow for the cost of your own time plus incidental expenses such as phone calls, travel costs, stationery and cleaning materials.

Step 3: Calculate how much your total investment will be
If you are considering whether to invest in a property, your investment will be more than just the basic cost of the property. You should also include *all costs associated with the purchase*, including mortgage fees, survey and legal costs. In addition, include any development, decoration costs and repairs you must do before you first let it out. If you are furnishing the property, you should include these costs too.

Also don't forget to count the cost of the money invested in the property from the time you bought it to when you first let it. This will be whatever interest your total investment could have earned elsewhere for the time from completion to first let as well as whatever interest your deposit money could have earned from exchange to completion.

In the previous example, where we were buying a property for £250,000, your total investment may look something like the details shown opposite.

So, the total cost or value of your investment is £256,937, a full 2.77 per cent more than the £250,000 basic cost of the property. Remember the calculation:

Yield = Total Rent minus Running Costs/Current Value of Property

When evaluating this example as a property investment, the figure that should go in the bottom half of the equation is £256,937 because this is the total investment that you, the buyer, will have to make.

Basic Cost of Property:	**£250,000**
Add	
Mortgage arrangement fee	£500
Solicitor's costs and expenses (including stamp duty land tax)	£3,350
Survey fee	£300
Cost of redecoration and fixing snags	£500
Cost of very basic furnishings	£1,000
Sub total	£255,650
Cost of money from completion to first let, say one month on £255,650 @ 5%	£1,065
Cost of utilities and council tax (though if unfurnished council tax will not normally apply for six months) up to first let	£150
Cost of deposit from exchange to completion, say 21 days on a £25,000 deposit @ 5%	£72
Total	**£256,937**

There are a few things you need to watch out for. You'll hear developers talk about very high and attractive yields on investment properties. Be careful, because when developers talk about yields some may be simply dividing the gross rent by the basic cost of the property. In other words, they ignore running costs and voids completely and don't take any account of the transaction and set-up costs you'll have to bear. By doing this, they make the yield seem much higher than it actually is.

Even worse, many investors and every property TV show I've ever seen fail to account for the opportunity cost of using the investors' own money. Let me explain.

In the example above I took as my starting point, the £250,000 basic cost of the property. Few in the buy-to-let mortgage market are going to lend 100 per cent of the value of the property — 85 per cent is normally the maximum that's ever been advanced, with the investor finding the remaining 15 per cent. In this example, you would need to put down £37,500 (15 per cent of £250,000) of your own money in order to buy this property, with the mortgage company putting up £212,500.

Some developers then simply divide the rent by the value of the mortgage loan. As this is much smaller than the total value of your investment, it again produces a much higher yield. It's possible to see how big a difference this makes. In our example, if you just take the basic £18,000 gross rent and divide this by the mortgage loan of £212,500, you get a "yield" of 0.0847 or 8.47 per cent!

However, if you subtract from your £18,000 gross rent, an allowance for a one month void each year of £1,500 as well as annual running costs of £2,000 and then divide this by your total investment cost of £256,937, you get what we could call a "true net yield" of about 0.056 or 5.6 per cent. £18,000 less £3,500 (£1,500 + £2,000)/£256,937 = 0.056 or, expressed as a percentage, 5.6 per cent.

This true net yield is obviously very much smaller than

the 8.47 per cent figure some would have you believe! Also, bear in mind in this example, if you used an agent to find a tenant, your total running costs are likely to be higher than £2,000 a year.

As long as the true net yield is greater than whatever the cost of borrowed money is to you, then you're making money on renting. In our example, the true net yield is 5.6 per cent and if the cost of mortgage money is 5 per cent, we are 0.6 per cent to the good. Put another way, 0.6 per cent of the value invested in the property (£256,937) is about £1,542, so this is what we are making in net income from the property.

Of course, if mortgage interest rates go up above 5.6 per cent, then, in this example at least, we will be making no money in net income at all. However, over time, if you have bought wisely you would expect rents to rise, thus increasing the income from a property in the future.

So, if you are investing in property you need to allow for the possibility that interest rates can go up and you must make sure that you can afford to meet interest repayments.

The key messages of this discussion about yields are:

- Be very sceptical about what anyone tells you about the rents they think they can achieve for a property – especially if they want to sell you a property or let it for you.
- Be realistic about *all* your costs – both the running costs and the transaction and set-up costs of a property investment.
- Be aware that many people misunderstand or mislead when they talk about yield. Do your own sums!

How to calculate capital growth

Of course, the other way that properties make money over time is by going up in value, or "capital growth". Fortunately, calculating this is easy. It's simply the difference between the value of the property when you buy it and the value when it's sold less the total costs incurred in buying and selling.

In the example above, the total buying cost (including mortgage cost, solicitor's, survey, furnishing and all preletting costs) is £256,937. In the same way, when a property is sold, it's important not to forget to include solicitor's costs, selling agent fees, costs in making the property ready to sell and the cost of utilities and lost rent from the day your last tenant leaves until completion.

Often, a property that has been let for a long time can look tired so, when the final letting ends, it's worth spending some money to make it look attractive to a potential buyer. I will discuss in Chapter 5 how to get the property to look its best. Don't forget to allow for this cost.

Don't forget about tax either. Most income on residential property is subject to income tax, and capital growth may be subject to capital gains tax. For more on taxes see Chapter 11.

Many people today invest in properties where the starting net yield is nil or negative. In other words, their running costs, including interest are higher than the expected rent. These people are hoping for better rents in the future, lower borrowing costs and good capital growth. But is this wise?

Well, it all depends. If you've done your homework, and follow my advice in Chapter 3, you'll have a good idea of whether future rents will be higher and if the property is going to go up in price. I think such a strategy can work, but some degree of caution and a long time-horizon are required.

Of course, yield and capital growth go together like a horse and cart. If the price of a property shoots up over time (high capital growth) but the rental income from the property stayed the same, then the yield must have gone down. If the yield goes low enough, then it's always worth thinking about selling and doing something else with the money, like investing in another area or even just putting it in the bank. If you put it in the bank though, you'll miss out on any further capital growth there might be in the property. Also, if you sell, you'll have to consider possible capital gains tax complications. Again, for more on tax see Chapter 11.

So, good professional landlords are always evaluating their property investments, looking at their potential, working out the best time to buy and sell and the best types of property to invest in. It is this that is the subject of the next chapter.

3

HOW TO FIND THE RIGHT PROPERTY

Location, location, location:
How to choose the right area

I became a property millionaire by focusing on buying into the right locations before they got discovered by others.

Location is extremely important when buying any property, and even more so when buying property as an investment. If you are buying to let, remember you aren't going to be living in it, your tenants are. So, if your idea of a superb location is somewhere on the moors, miles from main roads and public transport, you'll need to think again because such a location is very unlikely to appeal to many tenants.

Buying a property to suit themselves rather than their tenants is a common mistake that inexperienced landlords make. And it extends to the way they furnish their properties too, in that they tend to put in furnishings they like, which are often too expensive for tenants, when "clean and simple" is what usually works best.

The ideal property for letting is one that will give a

good rent and will have potential to go up in price too, in other words good income (or yield) and good capital growth. To achieve good yield we need to find areas (and types of properties within those areas) where there are lots of people looking to rent but not enough rented accommodation available of the type tenants are looking for. For the price of the property to go up, the area (and type of accommodation) must become more attractive to both home-owners and tenants.

The papers are full of tips for which areas are going to do well. Some of these will be good tips. However, if a journalist is writing about an area, it has probably "come up" quite a bit already and you may have missed out on being there at the beginning. "Ah," you think, "If only we had bought in London's Shoreditch before all the young and happening new media people moved in. If only we had spotted that second-home owners were driving the rapid growth of property prices in coastal towns. If only!"

Well, if you missed out on these opportunities you shouldn't punish yourself too much. Being in at the very start of an area's regeneration is the property investment equivalent of buying tech stocks – you could be lucky or you could be very unlucky. The fact is that these areas were once real wastelands and, to get in at the start, you would have been banking on a lot of things happening together. You would have been hoping that all those big office developments would really happen, that the Government would really build that transport link and the council would put in those major improvements to the environment and schools.

Experienced property investors with large property portfolios are able to risk investing in such "frontier" areas. But it is risky. If you're more inexperienced, look to find areas that not only have existing potential, but where future improvements are *really* coming – not just promised. In other words, that area of derelict land close by *really will* be built on and bring two thousand jobs and the green light *really has* been given for the diggers to move in and start work on the new tram link.

To get this information try to get up-to-date with what is going on in the local area. Good sources of information are the UK's regional development agencies, local council planning departments, local newspapers, libraries and estate agents. Appendix 2 gives details of good websites containing local information. Many of these show the actual prices that other properties sold for which is an excellent tool to use in your negotiations.

If you know that a local haulage site is going to become attractive housing, then the value of neighbouring property should go up too.

Talk to local people. They'll tell you all about local schools, crime and the efficiency of the council. Look around at different times of day and at night. Do the streets become rat-runs at rush hour? Is it a no-go area full of drunken hooligans at night? Is it under a flight path or next to a busy depot that starts at 4 am? Is it close to a sports stadium with all the problems of parking and rubbish on match day?

Try to imagine what the area will look like in the future and think about the risk of over-supply. What plans are there for other housing developments? Your new two-bedroom flat with a canal view might be in high demand in a newly attractive city centre when there are only two hundred other two-beds. What about where there are twenty thousand two-bed flats all competing with yours for a finite number of tenants?

Once you have found an area with good potential, develop good relationships with estate agents and treat them with professional respect so they call you when they have a property that suits your needs.

To let well the property must be close to local transport. Most tenants will rely on it at some time and few tenants are prepared to walk more than half a mile to the nearest station or bus stop; and the route should be well lit and safe. Property further away will achieve lower rents and take longer to let. Tenants also like to be close to shops, bars, restaurants and, if they have children, good local schools. With more up-market lets, being close to an international school can make a significant difference.

How to choose the right kind of property

Once you've spotted a good area, you have to buy the kind of property that meets tenant demand in that location. There's no point buying a big family house, if there's little demand for big family houses to rent!

Suppose you buy a big property and your target market is visiting families from overseas who want to be close to the local American school. You need to ask: Is this really a big enough market? How many families are there looking for properties like this in this area? Will the school be there forever? If not, would other families rent it? Could you let it to student sharers instead?

Letting agents know what kind of property is most in demand in an area. They'll tell you what sort of properties let easily and what they are most short of. Advice from agents who only do lettings (i.e. don't sell houses) is best because what they tell you won't be biased by any desire to sell a similar property to you.

Talk to letting agents
In 2003/4, the UK saw a big increase in the number of migrant workers – particularly from the new EU countries in eastern Europe. Government statistics don't show the true numbers and the media only picked up on it about two years after the first big influx but letting agents were well aware of it as soon as it happened. One letting agent told me that people from Lithuania and Poland made up about 60 per cent of his tenants. These groups have given a huge boost to private letting across the UK.

Even before you buy, you can assess the level of demand by putting a "test advert" in your local paper or property website advertising a fictitious property to rent. From the number of people who call you'll know the level of demand. If there was no interest, test the advert again, this time with a lower rent. Was there more demand this time?

Suppose you have identified a strong demand for two-bed properties. What kind of two-bedroom property is best? You could go for a house or flat, leasehold or freehold, purpose-built or conversion. How does an ex-council property sound? Which is better – a new-build or an older property? Very often, within a specific location, you may not have a choice.

Some investors talk about "buying for yield" or "buying for income", meaning the property has a relatively low price, will give a good rental income but probably won't go up in price too much. The classic "income" or "yield" properties are flats above shops which are often priced low because lots of owner occupiers don't want to live above a shop but, as long as it's attractive, safe, close to transport, etc, then it will probably rent quite well. In my opinion, such a property could give good yield and capital growth together because there is no reason why such a property shouldn't also go up in price. True, it will be slightly less marketable to buyers, but it will still sell, especially to other landlords.

Buying above a shop

If you buy above a shop, check whether the type of shop can change under the terms of the lease. A flat above a shoe shop is more saleable and rentable than one above a kebab shop! Also, check the HMRC website about the "Flat Conversion Allowance" which gives investors tax breaks on turning flats above shops back to residential use.

Yields on ex-council houses are also good. Such properties can usually be bought at prices below other equivalent-sized ones. Provided that the area itself is safe and the property attractive, they tend to rent well. Many tenants like the fact that most council flats often have larger room sizes, better sound proofing and greater storage space than conversions and modern purpose-built blocks and they are therefore prepared to pay more in rent for them. Good capital growth is often achieved especially in developments where there is a high (and increasing) proportion of owners relative to council tenants. Service charges also tend to be lower because the local authority is *usually* not out to rip off the leaseholders. However, be aware that some mortgage companies will not lend on certain types of ex-council properties.

The lowest net yields tend to be on flats in "mansion type" blocks. The effect of all that free hot water, porters and lift maintenance will be felt in high service charges, which will dramatically hit your net yield.

Until recent years it used to be the case that smaller properties generally yielded more than larger ones. However, in the last few years more families have started to rent. With a shortage of suitable properties, this has pushed up rental yields on houses above that achievable on flats in many areas. For the same reason, prices of houses have also risen faster than flats in most areas since 2001.

This shows how you need to keep up-to-date with demographic changes and housing supply. Alternatively, if you want to buy lots of property you could cover your bets by building a portfolio of different types of properties!

Parking facilities will be relevant where tenants or their visitors have cars. If the property has no parking space it should be easy and safe to park in the street. Tenants also like bright airy properties so, if it's summer, think about what the property will be like in winter. If all the windows face north it could be cold and dark. Watch out too for basement or ground-floor flats: these may be harder to rent out (and later sell) than flats on the first floor because of security concerns and because they're often gloomy! Some people won't rent above the second floor if there is no lift.

If you're interested in a particular road or area, try advertising privately to find people who live there and who may want to sell. You could also try leafleting the houses in the street(s) you are keen on. Make it clear that, as a private buyer, the seller will save on paying estate agent commission or auction fees.

If you see a derelict property you like, find out who owns it from the Land Registry website (see Appendix 2).

If this fails, the neighbours might know who is looking after it and you could approach them. If the owner has died, the heirs might be interested in selling privately.

Which is best: Leasehold or freehold?
What questions should you ask?

Where you own the freehold, you own the land on which the property sits too. If you have a flat, however, it's probably leasehold, and you are effectively buying the right to occupy space between the bricks in your part of the property, including, possibly, part of the garden.

I said "right to occupy," but really you effectively own it. In a typical lease of say ninety-nine years, you usually have the right, for a fee, to extend the lease or join with other leaseholders to buy the freehold or obtain the right to manage.

The lease document will contain a list of obligations on you (the leaseholder) and the owner of the building (the freeholder.) The freeholder (or his managing agent) will charge you ground rent and service charges, and it's normally his responsibility to look after the maintenance of the building, arranging the buildings insurance, etc.

If everyone involved did what they were supposed to do, it would all work well. Leaseholders wouldn't annoy other leaseholders and they would pay their ground rent and charges on time. The freeholder would properly maintain the property, insure the building, not rip off the leaseholders and do everything to ensure things ran smoothly.

Where it works well, there are financial benefits for the flat-owning leaseholder in that the cost of exterior decoration, buildings insurance and garden maintenance will be less than they might otherwise be in an equivalent size freehold property.

It can, and often does, work like this. Millions of people are leaseholders and, in cities, living in flats is often the only option. However, nearly every newspaper will have a column in their property supplement where frustrated leaseholders (and some freeholders) seek advice from the paper's solicitor on how to solve some problem or other with the working of their lease. Their questions are usually about how to get a freeholder or managing agent to do something they should be doing anyway, how to stop other leaseholders from doing things they shouldn't, how to extend a lease, buy the freehold or take over the management.

The fact is there are quite a few flats – especially conversions – where the building is managed badly. Typical problems are noise, crumbling exteriors and filthy common areas. Given that the law on leasehold has changed frequently in the last twenty or so years suggests it needed fixing. Things today are better than they were, but for many leaseholders there are still problems.

Although lots of leaseholders have problems with the management of their block, with other leaseholders or with the freeholder, many take no action because they know that, if they did, they would then be legally required to tell potential buyers as part of the pre-contract sale enquiries. So, if you're buying a leasehold property, you need to be particularly careful. Here are some tips.

Before even putting in an offer, find out how many years are left to run on the lease and what the ground rent/service charges are. If the lease has fewer than seventy five years left to run, many mortgage companies won't offer a mortgage. Extending a lease or buying the freehold gets considerably more expensive from when the lease has less than eighty years left. Since short-lease properties are hard to sell, because of the difficulty getting a mortgage, you'll need to pay to extend the lease sooner than with a longer lease. A short lease should be reflected in the asking price of the property.

Obtain a copy of the lease as soon as possible. Check it carefully and have your legal adviser do likewise. Are there proper provisions and arrangements for collecting ground rent and service charges? Is it clear who is responsible for the maintenance and redecoration of communal hallways, exterior walls and gardens? Is there a planned schedule for doing this? When was it last done? What state are the communal areas, gardens and exterior in? Are communal areas used as a dumping ground for rubbish? Is it clear who is responsible for arranging the buildings insurance? Are there any restrictions or charges levied where the property is let out? Are there likely to be major building or repair costs in the future? How involved are residents? Is the managing agent a member of the Association of Residential Managing Agents (see Appendix 2)? If it's a new-build, but a similar block has already been completed, talk to residents living there. What do they say? Are they plagued by noise or rude and inconsiderate neighbours? What is security like? What is the attitude of other residents to security? What is the ratio of owner occupiers to tenants?

With a flat, it's particularly important to visit at different times of the day and night, and especially when people in an upstairs property are in. Many flats with stripped wood flooring are unbearably noisy. (This is a particular problem with older conversions.) Find out before you buy!

Where a flat has joint share of the freehold, the freeholder's responsibility will be shared with others. Someone (and it may be you) has to arrange for moneys to be collected, insurance arranged and redecoration carried out. Where your flat alone owns the freehold, it will be you doing this.

The trouble with communal hallways

When buying a flat with a communal hallway, try to check out what sort of people live in the block and what the arrangements are for access and delivery of post. With communal hallways you sometimes get people leaving rubbish bags, bikes, etc. (If you suffer from this, go through the rubbish and see if you can identify the culprits, then get the managing agent to send them a warning letter.)

Other problems with communal hallways are lack of security – some people let anyone in and leave communal doors unlocked. If post is left in insecure communal areas either it can be stolen or people can have their own identity stolen.

Be careful too, when buying a newly built leasehold flat in a new development. Developers tend to underestimate what service charges will be in order to sell. Be realistic and remember that the nice swimming pool and gym have to be paid for somehow. Ask yourself whether the additional rent will be sufficient to cover adequately the cost of the gym, etc, which you'll be paying for in service charges. Usually, the answer will be no.

Recent changes in the law have brought in another option called "commonhold". This allows leaseholders, provided that certain qualifying criteria are met, to take over the management of their blocks without buying the freehold or proving that the freeholder is at fault, by simply serving the appropriate notice on the landlord. There will be a responsibility to file annual accounts so a commitment to make self-management work is crucial. As agreement from each person's mortgage company is also needed to covert to commonhold, unsurprisingly the rate of take up has been abysmal.

My very annoying freeholder

Every year or so, the freeholder of one of my leasehold flats writes to me and says: "Mr Lawrenson, It has come to our attention that your flat is being let out. As you know, as a leaseholder this requires approval from us. Please fill in the form attached and send it to us along with the requisite cheque for £79.95."

My response letter reads as follows: "Dear Mr Freeholder, Thank you for your letter. I'd be grateful if you would kindly point out where in the lease terms and conditions, it refers to the need for a leaseholder to (a) inform you of a subletting and (b) pay you £79.95 for this service. Please send me a cheque for £40.46, this being the cost of my time to write this letter and the cost of a first-class stamp."

Needless to say, that is the last I hear of him for a year or so. Is he making a genuine mistake or is he just trying to extract money where it's not due? I don't know and don't really care. It is just one of the hassles of being a leasehold flat owner!

Unfortunately, it's beyond the scope of this book to look in detail at leasehold or how to solve specific lease-hold problems. In fact it would require another book! If you have problems with a leasehold property contact the

Leasehold Advisory Service (see Appendix 2) which provides a wealth of advice for free.

At the end of this discussion, I'd say that although I have both freehold and leasehold properties, I much prefer the greater simplicity of my freehold houses. I like running my own show and think that, despite recent changes in the law, it's still difficult and expensive to enforce your rights as a flat owner when things are not working as they should. I'd rather that it's down to me to decide when the exterior needs redecorating and which company should insure it without reference to anyone else. Maybe that's just me being a grumpy sod?

Despite this, it must be said that leaseholds can be good investments, and hassle free − provided that everyone involved meets their responsibilities in the lease contract in full. It's up to you to check this is the case *before* you buy.

Whether to buy a new or old property: Things to consider

In the lettings market, it doesn't really matter whether the property is new or old. Some tenants prefer old properties, some new, but what they all like is space.

Brand-new properties can be problematic because they sometimes have lots of snags, things that need fixing that you only become aware of after moving in. In fact, one of the biggest buying agents has said he'd never buy a newly built property for this reason!

Many new properties these days seem to have quite small rooms and little storage space. Some developers and agents try to cover this up by dressing out their show houses with the tiniest furniture, televisions, refrigerators and dishwashers. If you're thinking of buying new, watch out for this trick.

If buying on a new development, check out what building work will be going on nearby as lots of noise will upset your tenants. If you know the waste ground opposite will be a building site for a while, be honest and tell your prospective tenant upfront.

If buying an older property look closely. Don't be afraid to look for signs of damp or mould under carpets and behind cupboards and consider getting a fuller survey than the standard "valuation report" that mortgage lenders tend to use. But use your judgment here – if the property looks in good condition and there are no visible signs of anything wrong structurally, you might just be OK with a basic valuation report. If you do go for a fuller survey, ask the surveyor specifically to check anything that particularly worries you and get a builder in so you can budget for building costs. Watch out too if you are thinking of developing or extending an older listed property as it may be impossible to get planning permission.

How to buy in new developments and off-plan (and avoid the pitfalls)

In recent years there has been a newly rediscovered desire to live in the centre of towns. The attractions are obvious. After a long tiring day you can just walk from the office to home in a few minutes without a long stressful commute. Builders have been busy putting up apartments in city and town centres throughout the land to meet the demand. Wine bars and restaurants have followed to make living in the middle of things more and more attractive.

Investors who bought years ago in many new-build city centre schemes have undoubtedly made a lot of money. In many cases they bought months or years in advance of completion. Many will have kept the properties and let them out but others will have sold on even before they were completed.

In some cases, the developer may have finished an identical existing block, so you'll know what your property will look like. In other cases, your property may be the first to be built. Either way, if it's not been built yet, you're buying "off-plan".

Most developers ask for a small initial non-refundable goodwill deposit, with the balance of the deposit – typically 5 or 10 per cent or £10,000 per unit – payable a few weeks later. Negotiate hard on the goodwill deposit because at this stage you won't know all the facts, like whether a huge ugly Tesco's is going to be built just opposite! The attraction is that once you've paid all the deposit it will be some time before you have to pay the balance on the property. However, even where your intention is to sell on before completion, you must still ensure that you can get a mortgage, just in case you can't sell on for whatever reason.

In a rising market, it's easy to see how people can make money out of buying new-build properties. Suppose you're buying a flat that is valued at £200,000, and the deposit is 5 per cent – i.e. £10,000. Suppose also, after twelve months when the property is nearly completed, it's risen in value by 10 per cent. The new valuation should come in at £220,000, so you'll now have £30,000 equity in the property. (Your £10,000 plus a £20,000 gain in value.) You could sell the property on, and your only outlay will be the £10,000 initial deposit plus interest, legal and agency fees for selling the property. There may be some liability for capital gains tax unless you can convince the Revenue that you should be classified as a property trader but stamp duty land tax will not be payable if the property is sold back-to-back before completion date.

Get a good solicitor
If you are buying off-plan and selling on before completion, find a good solicitor who understands the principle of back-to-back sales.

There are of course a few pitfalls with this, the most obvious one being that prices won't increase by 10 per cent and another that you actually paid too much for the property in the first place.

How does new-build and off-plan work? A lot of the developer's costs are upfront – he's got to get planning permission and then fund all the initial building and marketing. To do this he needs to raise cash as soon as possible. The problem is that many people won't buy until they can actually see something – and it may be some time until the show apartment is ready. Fortunately, for the developer there are a lot of investors who will take the risk of buying upfront and off-plan. This is particularly attractive to the developer if he can sell multiple units to a single buyer. The development is therefore often marketed to investors through buying clubs/syndicates who buy on behalf of individual investors, through buying agents/finders as well as through estate agents.

The buyer club, syndicate or agent is supposed to negotiate with the developer to get big discounts on a number of properties in a development on behalf of its members in exchange for a fixed fee levied on its members – typically 1 to 2 per cent. If you join a buying club or syndicate, the key is to satisfy yourself that the deal is sound and that you have got a genuine discount off the true value of the property. If you've got a discount off the price of an overpriced property, you don't have a good discount at all! Most developers tend to overvalue their developments so watch out for this.

To ensure that you've got a good discount get an *independent* valuation from an independent valuer, not one who is linked to or recommended by a buying syndicate or a developer. Bear in mind that the valuation of new-build is quite imprecise, as there may be little similar property to compare with. Even where there are comparables, each development will have its own specification, making it difficult to compare. Don't be afraid to quiz the valuer on how he arrived at the valuation. It's thought that some valuers don't want to disrupt the sales process and pass anything within 5 per cent of the true value as a fair asking price!

Will you get a mortgage?

Some mortgage companies now refuse to lend on new build or even anything less than two years old and all now require higher deposits. Others set limits to the number of buy-to-let mortgages that they'll offer on a single development so watch out for this if you hope to buy multiple units in the same block.

With new-builds, it's even more essential that you check out how many properties will be built locally in the next few years. Many inexperienced investors have found out that their property is just one of thousands of others, all competing for that same buyer or tenant. As a result, the capital growth and rental return performance of many new-build inner city flats has been poor, especially over the years from 2000 to 2008.

If there is a block of derelict land opposite, get your solicitor to check out with the local authority Planning Department what will be going in on that site – don't take the developer's assurances on this. I have heard buyers being told that the site opposite would be developed with a few small shops, when a huge superstore was planned.

Will your development be a tenants' ghetto? Where too many properties in a single development are sold to investors the price of the properties may fall in time. Most people, tenants included, want to live in blocks where there is some degree of permanence not one full of potentially transient tenants. In my consultancy work advising private clients I have seen many examples of blocks where more than a third of the units were let out and because absentee landlords were not around to push the freeholder, the blocks, car parks and gardens had descended into a dreadful state with no one around to fix the snags. So find out who is buying.

Check out the service charges carefully. Most developers are highly optimistic about how low service charges will be. If no properties have been completed yet, I'd add 50 per cent onto the service charges the developer quotes. If some blocks have already been completed and occupied for a few months, add on a third. You can get an idea of what service charges are locally by asking a local independent letting agent. Better still, if some of the development has already been completed, don't be afraid to knock on a few doors and ask the residents if they are happy with the service they're getting for the charges they pay. If there is a gym, pool or car park, you could stop and ask people there.

Find out what car parking will be provided. Will your target market need parking spaces? If it's not available and parking is on the street, how safe is it? Many new off-plan developments are in trendy inner city areas which have what many property writers call an air of "grittiness" to them. Basically, this means they aren't the sort of places you'd like your granny to walk around in at night and a smart car is likely to be a target for local ruffians. If it's too rough, many people will be put off renting there.

Ignore any rental yields quoted by the developer. Check out the local lettings market carefully with independent letting agents and via test adverts in papers. Take away 25 per cent from the rent that an agent says can be achieved to get a rental figure that will let it quickly and allow for at least a month before you get the first rental away.

Some buying agents and syndicates will offer to do the furnishing, letting and management for you too. See if you can do this part of the work cheaper or more effectively by arranging it elsewhere or doing it yourself.

Despite all these concerns, you can still do well buying new-build and/or off-plan. Indeed, some investors who "got in" back in the early days of inner city development have made a fortune. These people know their market well. They fully research the area and have a good picture of all new up-coming developments locally so they know to avoid areas where there will be an over-supply of properties. They also know all about planned regeneration schemes and new infrastructure.

They buy at times when the developer is most likely to give good discounts, which is often a few months before the developer's year-end or mid-term results, when the developer needs every sale it can get to show good results to the City. Buying at first release is also good – some developers will offer good deals to help their financing. At the end of a development, the developer may also give good discounts in order to hand over to the management company and cut site security costs. Most developers are publicly quoted companies and it's easy to find when their year end is.

Many developers offer sweeteners like guaranteeing the rent for a year or two or paying the stamp duty land tax. This makes good marketing copy but it often hides the fact that the property itself is overpriced. Also, where a developer guarantees to pay rent, the development is likely to end up mostly let out to tenants. Watch out too because guaranteed rental yields are worked out on just the basic cost of the property – i.e. with no added carpets, furniture or transaction costs.

Experienced investors will be able to disassemble these sweeteners. They'll know if the rent guarantee is worth having and usually prefer to negotiate on the basic price with all the sweeteners stripped out. You should do the same.

Many new development schemes these days are what are called "mixed tenure" developments, meaning there'll be a mix of "affordable [i.e. social] housing" and private property. Where this is so, check exactly what sort of affordable housing it will be. If it's a "shared ownership" where people will be part mortgaged and part renting from a social housing organisation, this is better than where they are fully renting. Where it's a shared ownership scheme, the owners will have at least a 25 per cent stake in the property and will look after it as well as full owners. I would be wary of buying where the social housing residents had no ownership or were not 'key workers'.

> *Check floor plans*
> As part of the legal process, obtain the floor plan for the property you are buying. Check size, dimensions, layout and outlook and compare with the show flat. Is it as good?

Finally, a word about buying agents and property syndicates. One reason people use them is to save time. The idea is that they'll find good deals for you so you'll save shoe leather. This is partly true. However, you must do at least *some* of your own research too. Satisfy yourself that the property is a good investment and it's in a good location. Ask questions!

Many buying agents and property syndicates are very good. Some aren't. Ask how long they've been in business, what references they can give you, how experienced the directors are, what guarantees there are, whether they are robust and what would happen if they went bust. (Usually you will lose your money!) Check out their accounts at Companies House (see Appendix 2). If you don't understand accounts, get someone who does to look over them for you. What does it say about them on the Internet? Do they have an open forum where past investors are free to post comments?

In my view the better buying syndicates are those where they have actually used their *own money* to buy property in bulk from a developer and then sell on. At least, you'll know they've put their own neck on the line financially. Others are just "introducers" who are just using your money and that of other people to negotiate a good deal from developers on bulk purchase.

More tips for buying off-plan and new-build

When buying new property use a developer that is a member of a recognised guarantee scheme. With some of these it can mean that if during the course of construction the developer goes out of business, the deposit paid by the buyer (up to 10 per cent of the agreed price) will be refunded. Also, during the first two years the developer should pay the cost of putting right damage or defects if these arise from a failure to follow the Scheme's building requirements.

If there are lots of things wrong with your new-build, consider employing a professional snagging company. Look on the Internet under "snagging companies".

Get an idea of the sturdiness of the construction by jumping up and down in the middle of the room. If pictures fall off the walls, take that as a bad sign! If possible, get a friend to go into the flat upstairs and make some noise. Can you hear every footstep?

If you want to buy quickly, see if the developer will agree to a deposit back clause in the event the property isn't ready in a certain timescale.

If you want to sell on the property before completion, check that the developer will allow you to do this.

Many off-plan buyers find that once they have bought the property their friendly property developer is totally uninterested in how the block will be managed in the future. In some cases, no managing agent has been appointed at all; in other cases, he is impossible to contact. See the section on "Lease or Freehold" above for the list of questions you should ask about this before you buy.

Whatever you do, don't be pressurised to sign up on the day to get a special deal. There are many deals out there. Don't waste lots of money going to seminars or pay upfront before exchange of contracts. Be especially wary where a syndicate wants you to use its own mortgage firm, valuer or solicitor.

Since syndicates are inevitably made up nearly entirely of people looking to sell on before completion or to let out, where a syndicate is buying multiple units in a new development there will be a lot of competition from other landlords for tenants. Rents will be much lower as a result.

If a syndicate claims that it can get a discount on a new-build property, find out if the developer will sell direct. If he does, ask what discount he would give you. How does that compare with what the syndicate or agency claims it could get? Finally, remember that buying agents, clubs and syndicates are not regulated by the Financial Services Authority and there is currently no recourse to a professional body. The glossy brochure may promise a profit, but it's not a guarantee.

How to buy at auction

Buying at auction has become more popular in recent years and many properties sold this way are bought as investments, either to rent out or do up and sell on. You can get a good bargain at auction but you need to know what you are doing. If you're serious about buying this way go to a few as a spectator first before getting involved yourself. Forthcoming auctions are advertised in local newspapers, the Internet (see Appendix 2 for address of useful website) or in the *Estates Gazette* magazine.

Prices at auctions may seem low, but often there is a

good reason. The properties may be in poor condition, have subsidence, be blighted by proposed road developments, been occupied by squatters, have sitting "Rent Act" tenants or have defects in the legal title. Or they may just be unique and hard to value.

Others may have nothing wrong with them at all other than possibly being in a mess. This is usually the case with ex-government housing, those being sold by executors after the death of the owner, repossessions and "distressed sales" where a property is being sold by people who have overstretched themselves.

The benefit of buying at auction is that you can get the property you want quickly without lots of negotiation. Once the gavel goes down, that's it! Provided that you are the highest bidder and your bid has matched the vendor's minimum price, the "reserve price," then it's yours.

It sounds simple and it is! The drawback is that, to be on the safe side, the buyer ought to have the property surveyed, mortgage ready and the bulk of the legal checks done *before* the auction. This all costs money, of course, but means if defects turn up and it wasn't worth what it sold for, then at least you will have avoided buying something that may have ended up being a nightmare. As with all property purchases it's really a case of "buyer beware"; if you don't check the property out carefully first and you find that it's falling to bits after you bought it, it's your problem.

How do you prepare for an auction? Ask for the package compiled by the auctioneer which should be available about four weeks before the auction. It will have details on each property and the memorandum of agreement which is equivalent to the contract, the title documentation, the searches, whether there are any

Tips for auctions

Some auctions quote a "guide price". It's not the same as the "reserve price" but it's a good indication. Typically, if the guide price is £75,000 to £85,000, the reserve price is probably around £80,000.

Ensure you have your deposit with you. Auctions won't take cash due to money laundering regulations. Check beforehand what form of payment is acceptable.

If you go with your partner, sit together. It's been known for a husband and wife sitting in different corners to bid against each other!

Be aware that the auctioneer, vendor or his agent can bid up to the reserve price without identifying himself. It's called "off the wall" or "imaginary" bidding and it's perfectly legal.

As soon as you buy, you're responsible for the insurance. Phone your insurer straightaway and get it covered. (Get quotes before the auction and remember that many insurers will charge more or won't insure at all where there is subsidence or if it's unoccupied.)

If the vendor is in a different part of the country from the solicitor it might be a probate sale. Often, the vendors will accept low prices in order to "move on" quickly.

Repossessions often have the words "for sale by mortgagee in possession" in the details. These are often left in a mess but if structurally sound can be bargains.

If buying with existing tenants in place, check what sort of tenants they are. Assured Tenants or Assured Shorthold Tenants might be OK but "Rent Act" Tenants should be avoided as the rent will be fixed at a low level and it will be virtually impossible to get them out. See Chapter 6 for more on the different types of tenancy contracts.

outstanding planning or environment issues, etc, and replies to general enquiries. Ideally, have this checked over by a conveyancer. Look out also for any special conditions. For example, it may say that the buyer has to pay the vendor's legal fees.

Then go and view it. Many have to be seen at block viewings, so you'll get to see possible fellow bidders.

Once you've found a property you like, recheck with your conveyancer that it's free from legal problems, in particular, that there is no problem with legal title.

If paying cash, since many properties sold at auction have structural problems, you'd be wise to get a fairly thorough survey done anyway. If it needs work, carefully budget for it with a good builder. The builder may want paying if doing the quote involves significant work but, if you get the property and he gets the work, the cost of the quote should be deducted from the cost of the work. Get fixed quotes (not estimates) and obtain a proper specification of the works to be done and what materials will be used (and ensure these are included in the cost). I'll say more about this in Chapter 5.

Before the auction, work out the maximum price you're prepared to bid. If you're the highest bidder and the reserve has been met, you must sign the contract in the auction room and pay a 10 per cent deposit.

You must complete twenty-eight days later, so your solicitor needs to move quickly and get all legal documents ready. If you don't complete, you lose not only your deposit but, if the property has to be re-auctioned and it ends up fetching less than you have paid, you'll be liable for the difference! So use a conveyancer who understands the auction process and can work fast!

On the day, arrive early, check the "addendum" and recheck the legal pack in case any special conditions have been added.

Auctions are very fast-paced events and each property sells very quickly so keep cool and stick to your maximum price. Don't go above it! Some auctions will have a reserve price stated. If it isn't, and the auctioneer says something like, "This property will sell today" or "It's in the room", this means that the reserve price has been reached and the highest bidder will get it.

If the sales details quote "unless previously sold" you should be able to approach the auction house and make a bid in advance of the auction. This will be conveyed to the owner who may accept it. You'll still need to move fast and ensure that the finance is ready and that the conveyancing can be done quickly.

If the property hasn't met its reserve, the auctioneer will tell you the reserve and advise if he has the vendor's authority to sell at the reserve price for up to twenty-four hours after the auction. Many pro investors actively pursue a strategy of snapping up bargains where the property fails to reach the reserve price.

Does everything work?
Things to check before you buy

Apart from your survey, you need to check the basics, such as whether the central heating, cooker and shower work properly, what the standard of plumbing and wiring is like, where access to the drains and mains fuse boxes are, the state of the roof and chimneys, whether the windows open properly, etc. If you have any concerns or are unable to check yourself, get a suitable professional to check for you.

> *Things to look for*
> Check where the water stop-valve, manhole and electricity fuse-board are – they may be in another property. If they're not somewhere accessible, it will cause problems when things go wrong. For example, a manhole cover is often covered with lawns or cement, but it's usually the point where blockages often occur. Try to get the vendor to make these things accessible before you proceed. If the vendor doesn't know where they are, the appropriate local utility company will be able to tell you.

How to negotiate successfully

If you've done your research, you'll know what the property is worth (and what you can receive in rent from a tenant). When you make an offer, allow for the vendor to come back with a counter offer by ensuring that your first offer is some way below your maximum.

If you're buying through estate agents, use them to help your negotiation. They are supposed to work for the vendor and get the best (i.e. highest) price. However, if you probe in the right way they'll usually tell you lots about the vendor's circumstances and what price he'll accept. For example, "The vendor is desperate to sell to meet his divorce costs/kids' school fees/new life and wife in Thailand and he will probably accept X." If the agent isn't very forthcoming, ask questions. Sometimes, junior staffers play it straight, giving little away to buyers. If this is the case, see if you can get more out of the branch manager.

If you're buying direct (i.e. with no agent) you will

have to negotiate direct with the vendor. This can be tough, especially when you've put in an offer well below asking price. Keep it professional, it's only money!

How hard you negotiate depends on how much you want it and how desperate the vendor is to sell. As an investor you can make some pretty hard offers and walk away if they don't come off. Remember: you're buying it as an investment not to live there! Eventually, someone will be keen enough to sell and will accept a low offer – this is especially true in times of economic crises when people are suffering financially.

If your negotiation gets stuck try asking the vendor to make some improvement or repair something broken in exchange for meeting his desired price. If you don't need to sell property to finance this one, keep reminding him that you can move more quickly than someone who is stuck in a chain.

The house market is seasonal with lots of buyers out in late spring and in early autumn too. If you want to buy property cheaply, it's probably best to avoid these times. There are a few people who don't like landlords, especially ones that come in with low offers on their cherished property! If the person you are buying from is like this, just tell him you're a buyer who is not in a chain. He doesn't need to know your intentions for the property.

If you're a cash buyer and not dependent on getting a mortgage, then use this in your negotiating position too. By not having to wait for a mortgage offer, you can cut the conveyancing process by at least two weeks. If the seller wants to move quickly, this will give you a significant advantage over other potential buyers.

In a busy market a vendor might ask potential

purchasers to put in "sealed bids" (rather like the "offers over" system in Scotland). However, the vendor doesn't have to accept the highest offer, so it's still worth reminding him that you aren't in a chain/are a cash buyer, so can move faster than other bidders or fit in with his timescales. In general though, as a property investor, you should avoid sealed bids situations in favour of finding willing sellers and building relationships with good estate agents so they eventually start calling you when a good deal comes along.

Buying below market value (BMV)

At property investor shows, seminars on how to buy property below market value (BMV) are now very much the flavour of the times with four or five operators running seminars.

Of course, any sensible property investor will always strive to buy cheaply. After all, the advantage you have as an investor is that if the vendor won't play ball, you can just walk away and wait until the next deal comes along. And clever investors have long recognised that to get really good value you have to find a "motivated" or "distressed seller" – someone who is motivated to sell to you at a good price for whatever reason.

And this strategy really just boils down to buying from someone who needs to sell fast – and often this means someone who is facing one or more of the three Ds – death, debt and divorce.

All good BMV practitioners have a system to generate a flow of "leads" coming in and a way of finding that special someone who will sell his property cheaply. They also use a number of techniques to drive potentially motivated sellers to them. One of these techniques is leafleting. This involves printing thousands of leaflets and having them dropped through letter boxes in the area you are interested in buying in. The message of these leaflets will be simple. "Do You Own Your Own Home? Do you need to Sell Quickly? Contact 0800 XXX." Another way is to advertise on the Internet – many of the two million sites that are returned when you key in "below market value property" are targeted at people who may be motivated sellers. Other techniques involve taking out adverts in the local press or radio.

It's all a lot of work, so some big players in the "below market value business" have now set up their own national network of sourcers of BMV property and call centres to field enquiries and filter out the genuine "distressed seller." They then sell these "hot leads" to investors who may then be charged for each lead that comes onto his patch.

Once he has found a potentially motivated seller, the investor will then usually call him and try to qualify him over the phone before arranging a meeting and setting up a deal to buy the property from him quickly for at least 20 per cent below its true value.

There are many below market buyers who use "bridging finance" to get the deal done without using any of their own money. Here's how it works. The investor finds a property worth say £200,000 but the owners want a quick sale and will sell for only £160,000. The investor will then raise a bridging loan for the £160,000 and complete the purchase. At the same time, he applies for a remortgage supported by a valuation for £200,000 on which he applies for a mort-gage of, say, £170,000 (85 per cent). This gives him "instant equity" to pay towards purchase costs, the cost of the bridging loan and the cost of his time finding the deal. This is, of course, very attractive to would-be investors who perhaps think property investment is a get rich quick scheme and want to get into it but don't have any deposit to put down. However, the credit crunch of 2008 forced mortgage lenders to stop doing "next day remortgages" and it remains to be seen if they will ever restart lending on these terms. Also, lenders have become wary of clever financial deals for novice investors and are now checking ever more carefully to see that there is real value in the property.

Some critics say the only people who are making any money out of BMV are the marketers of the schemes as they stand to gain from the seminars, from the supply of quality leads from their marketing and from the bridging loan finance too.

I think this is a bit unfair because it is possible to make money buying below market value, though it is not easy because it is very hard work to sift through thousands of leads in search of a good below market value deal and then to close the deal.

Some BMV solutions involve the vendor selling to an investor and then renting back the property from them – often called "Sale and Rent Back" (or SARB). This has the neat advantage that it allows the seller to continue living in his home with no adverse marks on his credit file. There are naturally criticisms of this from an ethical standpoint and many people see below market value investors as preying on people's misfortune and giving them little back in return. For example, where a distressed seller sells and rents back under an assured shorthold tenancy (the only type of tenancy a buy-to-let mortgage would allow) the seller-turned-tenant has no security of tenure after six months.

But BMV fans point out that many indebted people leave it too late and their circumstances are better served by a below market value operator because it means they can stay in their home rather than face being repossessed by their mortgage company. And from the sellers' point of view they won't have to pay estate agency fees and may also come out with some cash to hopefully get their lives back on track.

However, tales of people being ripped off by SARB operators on the sale price of their home and then being evicted once they are tenants are all too common, so legislation was passed which now requires operators to be authorised under the Financial Services Act. They now need to give "distressed sellers" more information about the true value of their property and their future rights as tenants. The new rules make SARB deals a lot harder to do and the compliance requirements will be too much for many operators.

At www.LettingFocus.com, I advise many people on the pros and cons of BMV deals. Whether you think BMV is right for you will depend on how much time you can devote to this and your attitude to the ethical issues involved.

In summary, finding and then persuading people to sell their property at say 20 per cent below market value is a time-consuming business. You need to be very patient and persuasive, and you need a team of sharp solicitors and mortgage brokers who understand clever financial deals and can act fast. But, in my opinion, unless you plan to be a full-time property investor you may do better by focusing on those geographic areas set to reap the benefits of regeneration or transport improvements – and then playing hard ball to buy property at least 10 per cent below asking price from local estate agents. (And don't forget that most repossessions go through estate agents first before they go to auction so find out which agents in your area deal with repossessed property.)

Finally, three last bits of advice. First, if you are after BMV deals and wish to pay a sourcing company for access to "hot leads", make sure you check out the company's past performance very carefully and find out how financially robust they are. Second, it is illegal to offer a bribe or inducement to an agent who is acting for a seller to give a buyer priority access to properties for sale and the agent must declare any conflict of interest to his client. Third, if you fail to declare the true price you are paying for a property on your mortgage application and if you "forget" to declare any discounts or side offers, you have committed mortgage fraud.

4

READY TO BUY: FINANCE AND THE LEGAL STUFF

Now you've found your property, you just need to ensure that your finance is all ready and you know what legal documents you and your conveyancer will need to check. This chapter will guide you through the finance maze and help you get the best from your conveyancer.

How to arrange your finance

Today, I do an increasing amount of consultancy with mortgage companies to help them improve their buy-to-let products and generally things are improving, albeit very slowly.

There are five things that bug me about mortgage companies.

Firstly, they rarely reward loyalty. Only a few of the more forward thinking lenders have products in place that meet the needs of the larger "portfolio" landlord.

Secondly, they have only just started offering lower interest rates for those landlords who borrow only a small proportion of the house value.

Thirdly, the tariff of ancillary charges that lenders levy for running a mortgage account gets ever longer and more punitive. "Lost your last mortgage statement and want a new one – that will cost you £50 sir." "Writing a letter to you, that will cost you £50 sir." "Closing your mortgage, that will be £100 sir." "A loan over 90 per cent loan to value – that will incur a special Mortgage Indemnity Fee, sir." If you are shopping for a new mortgage, ask the lender for their tariff of charges. If they're unjustified, go elsewhere and write and tell the lender's top boss why.

Fourthly, they never have enough staff. It doesn't matter how quiet the housing market is, some lenders seem not to have enough staff to answer the phone or process your application in a reasonable period of time.

Fifthly, some of the banks and other financial companies are the chumps who, by their reckless activities, caused the 2008 credit crunch for which we are all now paying in terms of higher mortgage rates, tightened lending criteria and reduced incomes.

Not all banks and building societies provide mortgages for landlords. However, there are plenty of lenders out there who do and many of these have specialist units. Obviously you don't need to restrict your choice of lender to the one who provided financing for your own home and you don't even need to be a home owner yourself or even to have had a mortgage, though it does help and an increasing number of lenders now require it.

Most lenders are not too interested in your income (though most will expect you to have a reasonable level of provable earnings), but they are interested in the potential rent. As a general rule, you'll need to put in at least 20 per cent of the property valuation from your own funds.

When the credit crunch eases off, you might, once again, be able to get a higher loan to value than 80 per cent but you'll pay a much higher interest rate and arrangement fee if you do.

If you're struggling to get the loan on your own, consider a co-mortgage, where up to four people can be on one mortgage and covered by a legal "deed of trust". Make sure you trust your co-owners because each of you will be jointly and severally liable for the whole mortgage!

Most lenders charge ever higher application fees for buy-to-let mortgages. Very irritating! These fees can normally be added to the mortgage itself, which means you pay interest on the fee you have paid to them to lend you the money in the first place. Great business this mortgage lending, isn't it?

In addition to the usual valuation, the lender will normally ask the surveyor to report what rent he thinks the property can achieve. The lenders will want the rent to be at least 1.25 times greater than the interest payments on the mortgage loan. So if your mortgage interest will be £1,000 per month, they would expect rental income to be 1.25 x £1,000, i.e. £1,250 per month. This "rent to interest" restriction often results in the amount of loan offered coming in at well below 80 per cent of the property valuation. So watch out for this.

If the survey values the property below what you've offered, go back and renegotiate with the vendor. However, if you've negotiated well already, you may not get much more off. If the survey is OK, then the mortgage should be approved and the legal process leading to contract exchange and completion can start.

There are many types of mortgage available, the main

choice being between fixed and variable rate ones. Fixed mortgages have the interest rate fixed for a limited period, usually one, three or five years. (Fixes for the entire life of the loan have proved unpopular in the UK.) After the fixed period, the rate reverts to the standard mortgage variable rate. A variant of the fixed mortgage is the "cap and collar" where the interest rate is fixed, for a time at least, between a lower and higher interest rate. The advantage of fixed rate products is that you'll know what your interest payments are going to be for the period of the fix, which can be quite reassuring.

Tips for arranging a mortgage

You usually have to pay the mortgage company to arrange a survey. They choose the surveyor and make additional profit by paying the surveyor less than you paid to them. Yes, it's just another way they make money! However, there are some that let you arrange your own survey. If so, you'll pay less than you would where the lender arranges it.

Even if you're a cash buyer it's still probably worth getting a survey if you're buying in an area with a history of subsidence or if the property is in poor condition. If you have real concerns, go for a fuller structural survey rather than the more basic "valuation report".

If you are letting it, you don't need to take out an endowment or life policy. If a lender tries to sell you one, go elsewhere.

Avoid making too many formal applications for mortgages as these all show up on your credit file, potentially worsening your credit rating.

Variable rate mortgages go up and down depending on prevailing interest rates. Discounted mortgages are a type of variable rate where there is some discount off the standard variable mortgage rate for a period of one, three or five years. After that, they also revert to the standard variable mortgage rate.

Watch out for early redemption penalties on fixed and discounted mortgages. These penalise borrowers who end the mortgage early, even if only moving to another mortgage with the same company. The penalty period often applies even after the fixed or discounted period has ended. So, for example, you might have a discount for a period of two years, but be penalised if you come out any time up to three or five years. Penalties can be quite high, so avoid products with penalties if you think you may wish to close the mortgage early.

I have to say that I usually go for variable rate mortgages over fixed rate ones because in my experience fixed rates usually look expensive compared to variable rate deals. This is just my preference though and, as I say, if you want to fix your outgoing interest payments for a time, then fixed rates may be better for you.

I also like "base rate tracker mortgages". With these, there is a guarantee that the mortgage rate will never be more than a set amount above the central bank (Bank of England) base rate. If the rate is not linked to the central bank rate, the company will be free to set any rate and call that "the standard variable rate". This might be uncompetitive and, if you're tied in, you may be stuck on a very uncompetitive rate indeed.

The other consideration is whether to go for an interest only or a repayment mortgage. With a repayment one, some of your payments go to pay off the loan outstanding, whereas with interest only mortgages, you just pay off the interest, leaving the amount borrowed the same. Which is best for you will depend upon your long-term objectives and cash flow position. Interest only or repayment mortgages can be combined with fixed, variable or discounted products.

Many professional landlords opt for interest only because interest on an investment property is currently deductible from rental income for tax. The problem with repayment mortgages is that the more you pay off from the capital, the lower the loan outstanding and interest become, so the more profit you'll potentially make on which you'll have to pay tax.

For example, if the rent is, say, £10,000, the interest is £7,000 and other costs are £2,000, then taxable income would be £1,000, i.e. £10,000 less (£7,000 + £2,000).

Mortgage brokers

In periods when mortgage finance is not constrained by credit crunches, mortgage lenders may have special discounted products that are only available through mortgage brokers so it might be worth considering approaching a broker. They advertise on the Internet and in local phone directories. Bear in mind though that they will usually charge a fee, which may cancel out any saving you make on the mortgage.

Mortgage brokers are especially useful for the self-employed or people who may have difficulty proving their income – in which case you may be offered a "self-certificated mortgage". They also know their way around each lender's criteria, so this may save you time if you or your proposed property are unusual in any way.

However, supposing you had paid off half the mortgage loan, then the interest would also fall by half from £7,000 to £3,500. If the rent is still £10,000 and other costs still £2,000, then taxable income would go up to £4,500, i.e. £10,000 less (£3,500 + £2000). With the higher income there would be more income tax to pay!

So, by keeping a lot of money borrowed, your interest cost can stay high and your taxable income will stay low. However, care needs to be taken not to have too much borrowing because, even with careful planning, things still go wrong – tenants can be hard to find, rents or house prices could fall and unexpected costs can crop up. Therefore keep borrowing reasonable.

It's useful to have flexibility either to make one-off capital payments or to take out additional mortgage funds without having heavy charges imposed on you for doing so. Check the mortgage provider's tariff of charges on this. Check, too, that all payments you make are applied to reduce the mortgage loan and interest payments immediately – this is sometimes called "daily interest calculation". (Unfortunately, there are still lenders around who only adjust payments and hence the amount of interest paid annually. This effectively means that money you have paid in earlier in the year is sitting in the lender's account making them rich but doing nothing for you!)

The better mortgage lenders can make additional advances on one property based on equity they know you have in another property, without going through the hassle of needing a valuation. This is obviously very convenient.

You may also be able to borrow money based on capital in your own home if you have one, or on another invest-ment property. Again, check the lender's fees for doing this. The interest rate may be lower if you have a good existing banking relationship with your existing lender (but don't bank on it).

Finally, if you want to let out your own home, you must ask your mortgage lender's and insurer's permission first. Even if they don't normally operate buy-to-let mortgages, they will usually be prepared to consider your request and "consent to let" although they may want a higher mortgage rate.

Each company has its own criteria, setting out what it will give a mortgage on and who they will lend to, based on the applicant's past credit history. These criteria have all been tightened up considerably as a result of the credit crunch. Also, some lenders will not lend on new builds, anything slightly out of the ordinary, such as a flat above a shop, in a big tower block or an ex-council house. Others will, so shop around.

Post the 2008 credit crunch, the margins that mortgage lenders want over bank base rates for lending you money have widened considerably. In 2007 it was possible, for a mortgage fee of just £500, to get a buy-to-let mortgage with a margin over Bank of England base rate as low as 0.7 per cent *for life*. It could be a long time before such rates reappear.

How to make the conveyancing process work for you

Once you've got your mortgage offer you can start the legal process leading up to completion and ownership of the property – what is called "conveyancing".

In England and Wales it typically takes about ten to fourteen weeks from when the offer has been accepted to when completion takes place. If you aren't relying on a mortgage, and can start the conveyancing process quickly, you should be able to shave at least two weeks off that.

In Scotland the process of buying and selling a property will be faster because contracts become legally binding once an offer is received and accepted. For more on the Scottish conveyancing system, see the box on page 221.

Lots of people complain about conveyancers. Common gripes are that they're too slow, they don't provide updates and don't return phone calls. Here are some tips to help you find a good one.

Ask friends and family and look for firms advertising on the Internet. If you ask friends, be careful to check that the person they used is still at the firm and ask your friend if he got on with the job quickly. This is important because if your friend wasn't in a hurry to complete, you won't know if the conveyancer can perform to a deadline.

Get quotes from a number of firms and be prepared to negotiate on fees. Ask about their quality of service. Ask if they have service standards to return phone calls within a specific period of time. The average conveyancer's heart will skip a beat at this as service standards and conveyancing firms aren't natural bedfellows!

Ask who will actually be handling your file and providing you with updates and how often. They will automatically say something like, "The partner, Mr X, will be handling your account personally." In reality, what happens in practice is that your file is delegated to a junior member of staff with the partner or other manager only checking the file at the end of the process and your initial call will be the first and last time that the partner actually speaks to you.

Can your conveyancer work to a deadline?

I once used a conveyancing firm on a purchase where the property was completed in Spring but the offer was accepted in October. I wanted to keep the process slow so I could avoid completing in November or December when the letting market tends to be quiet. It worked well. Completion was effected in mid February when there were lots of tenants looking and I was able to let the property quickly.

I then used the same firm for a property I wanted to sell quickly. It was only then that I noticed how slow they were. Most of my updates came from my estate agent and I had to push the solicitor all the way. I wouldn't use that firm again if I was in a hurry!

Ensure that you get a fixed fee, one that can't go up if things turn out to be more complicated than expected.

Some conveyancers will ask you to pay a fee towards their professional indemnity insurance. I find this a bit of a cheek. Their professional indemnity insurance is something they should have anyway, so I don't see why the client should have to pay for it. If they try this on, go elsewhere.

Get a written quote and make sure that everything is included, so that when comparing quotes, you know you are comparing like with like.

If you can use a local firm then this may help if time is of the essence and you need to drop off or pick up documents. It will also avoid the conveyancer making the "it's in the post" excuse! However, the cheapest firms can often be found by searching on the net using sites like www.reallymoving.com –and these may not be local.

So what do conveyancers do as part of the house purchase process? Here is a very quick guide. They'll look at the title deeds to check that the person you are buying from (and their mortgage company if applicable) is registered as the owner at the Land Registry. They'll check the questionnaire the seller has completed on the property about such things as if there have been any disputes, who pays to fix things like boundary walls, whether the gas, water, drains, electricity and phones are connected, what access is granted, whether any building work has been done and if so was planning consent obtained, whether there has ever been a change of use or alteration (e.g. to a conversion) and whether it has been approved and whether there are any guarantees that come with the property.

The questions will also ask if full vacant possession will be granted. (It is possible to buy a property with an existing tenant *in situ*, but you would need to ensure that the contract with the tenant allowed you to gain possession when you want to. For more on contracts see Chapter 6.) Where the property is leasehold, a separate form will be sent asking further questions about service charges and the like.

If you're buying, you need to check the answers carefully. If it's leasehold, look at the most recent accounts from the managing agent of the freeholder to see what costs have been incurred in the past. Look into whether there are any upcoming major works planned and what the cost will be.

The conveyancer will also check the local authority search information supplied. However, this won't tell you about planned developments a mile away. It's up to you to find this out from your own research of the area including your own checks with the Town Hall's Planning Department and other local estate agents.

Once everything is in place, the conveyancer will send a draft contract which basically states who is selling what to whom. The buyer hands over a deposit, usually 10 per cent of the value of the property. Contracts are then exchanged (normally via a phone call) which means you must complete on the purchase. If you don't, you lose your deposit.

Both buyer and seller should be sent a completion statement. For the buyer it will show the balance to be paid, including all costs and legal fees. Check it carefully against your initial quote. In particular, check if the conveyancer has deducted any amount you've already paid upfront from his final fee as I've found that most conveyancing solicitors are very adept at forgetting to do this. The buyer will be asked to have the money cleared and in his solicitor's account on completion day.

Homes marketed for sale on or after 21 May 2010 will no longer require a Home Information Pack (HIP) though the Energy Performance Certificate will be retained. Sellers will still be required to commission, but won't need to have received an EPC before marketing their property. Your solicitor should ensure the Energy Performance Certificate is available before exchange of contracts.

5

REFURBISHING AND PREPARING YOUR PROPERTY

How to deal with builders

If the property you bought requires some work to get it up to standard, you may need to employ a builder. If you're tempted to do difficult jobs yourself, remember that most jobs will take longer for you to do than they would a professional. As a property investor, when you have a big mortgage and no rent coming in, time really is money, so even if you can get it done cheaper doing it yourself, once you factor in the extra time taken you may not be really saving at all.

How to find a good builder? Start with recommendations. If you have friends who have had a job done on time and to a good standard, go and see it yourself. If it's a specific job such as roofing, check if he is a member of the trade body for that profession. Most trade bodies have a website or a phone number listed in local phone directories. Check with the trade body to see what guarantees (if any) a company's membership really gives you.

Find out how long the company has been in business and ask for proof that they possess the necessary liability insurance. Request references for previous work. Never agree to pay by the hour and always insist on a quote not an estimate. An estimate is nothing more than a rough guess of what the job might cost whereas a quote should be fixed and break down the work involved into distinct parts.

Prepare a detailed specification of the works you want done and be as specific as possible. Leave nothing to chance! Be clear whether it will be you or the builder who will pay for materials. If it's a big job obtain at least three quotes and ask each company to provide a description of materials and their cost. For big jobs, the quote should be itemised for each stage of the project.

Taking legal action against a tradesman

I've only once taken court action against a tradesman. It was against an electrician and as the amount was under £5,000 I went through the small claims court. NICEIC, their trade body, supported me in my claim. I won and the electrician had to refund my money plus the cost of the small claims action and the bailiff who was sent to enforce judgment. Claims over £5,000 can't go through the small claims court, so, it's even more essential on big jobs for you to check a tradesman's insurance and to have a proper contract.

Check the builder's availability and avoid those who'll be juggling your job alongside too many others. However, bear in mind, if they can't start right away, that might indicate they are in demand because they're good! So, if you want to buy a property which needs building work, get the builder in to quote as soon as possible, and well before exchange of contracts if it's going to be a big job. If you are buying a property, the builder must commit to start on completion day.

Assess how professional they were when they came to look at the job. Did they make lots of notes? Do you think you can get on with them? Did they treat you and your property with professional respect? Then go through each written quote in detail. Did they provide a breakdown of materials' cost and quote for everything in the job spec? Did they explain any technical jargon? Did they provide insurance certificates and agree to provide reference sites for other work? Did they commit to be available and say how long the job would take? Did they say who will supervise the work?

Are they planning to subcontract work? If so, how well do they know the people they'll be subbing to? It might be that they don't have, say, a good kitchen fitter on their books and therefore decline to quote for this part. This is not necessarily a negative thing or a problem. Provided that the part they can't do is self-contained, not interdependent with other work or at the end of the job, it might be worth employing a separate tradesman. Get references and quotes for any other tradesman you employ directly.

Don't just go for the cheapest quote but take account of everything. On a big job retain 5 to 10 per cent of the total cost for "snagging"; this to be payable one month after the job has been completed if there is nothing wrong. Retaining a small amount like this will ensure they come around promptly to fix any defects.

Agree a timescale in writing and don't be afraid of imposing penalties in the contract if they're late. However, you must accept delay if it's you who changes your mind. Builders make lots of money from the extra things you think of as the job progresses because once on the job they can control the price of the extras. That's another reason to be completely clear and have a detailed specification at the outset. So don't change your mind or add things in later!

You should both sign the quote or have a special contract drawn up. If the builder finds unforeseen problems along the way, then it's usually his problem as he should have checked out everything first. In some cases, however, it might have been impossible to have anticipated the problem. If in doubt or in dispute with your builder you could ask an *independent* surveyor for his opinion. It's worth putting in your contract something like "claims for unforeseeable work will not be entertained, where the work could reasonably have been anticipated".

Don't cheat the Revenue by paying in cash, as you'll have less come back if the job isn't done properly. A large builder (with a turnover of approximately £60,000 plus) will be registered for VAT, so at least you'll know that it is a large outfit. Smaller builders may keep under the VAT limit by asking you to pay for building materials and subcontractors' costs directly. There is nothing wrong with this, but remember to keep all receipts. Note that VAT will already have been charged on the building materials supplied, so there is no need to pay it twice.

If necessary don't forget to get planning permission and comply with building regulations (see below). Also, never pay until the agreed stage of the work has been completed, the only exception to this being where perishable or made-to-measure materials are needed. See also Chapter 8 for how to maintain a property once it's let and how to find a good plumber, gas engineer and electrician.

How to deal with architects and surveyors

If the job is too big or complicated, then consider employing an architect. Contact the Royal Institute of British Architects for help finding a suitable architect. If structural changes are proposed then you'll also need a structural surveyor, so get in touch with the Royal Institution of Chartered Surveyors. Contact details for both these organisations are given in Appendix 2. If your work involves a wall shared with a neighbour, you'll need to get him to sign up to a party wall agreement.

Seek recommendations from friends and talk to a number of architects. Ask for references, examples of previous work and fees. As for builders, agree a cost for the whole job not a by-the-hour-payment, and clearly set out what they'll do for you and whether they'll also project manage the work.

Where you are planning major works, a quantity surveyor might be worth employing. He can produce a "schedule of works" which is basically a detailed spec for the work. He can help you choose the right builder, compare quotes and set out payment stages. The builder should agree and sign a copy of the schedule of works. A building surveyor might be required to ensure that your builder has done the work to the right standards in accordance with current building regulations. Finally, if you are considering buying a property which has evidence of subsidence, it might be worth getting it checked over by a structural engineer. He can also advise on the consequences of making structural alterations.

How to get planning permission and building regulations approval

Depending on what you're doing, you may need to apply for planning permission. If so, phone the council for the planning forms and submit your plans and your fee. Tell the neighbours about your plans and try to get their agreement before you apply because the council will contact them anyway.

An architect or a planning consultant can handle the process of getting planning permission for you and meet the planning department too. He can also give an expert view of what would be acceptable to the planning department before you even apply. A simple alteration or extension should be passed (or not) within eight weeks but it will depend on your local office. (Some councils fail to take action against developers and businesses who ignore planning conditions. However, as a property investor, you'll one day hope to sell, so you have to be in compliance.)

Work must adhere to building regulations. The Buildings Regulations Officer at the local council planning office can send you their guidelines and application forms appropriate to the work you are carrying out. Once you've submitted the forms, a Buildings Officer will then visit to make sure the site complies with the guidelines.

If employing a builder, check that he has submitted the application forms because Buildings Officers have the power to shut down unsafe sites.

Once the work is completed, a Buildings Regulations Approval Certificate will be issued. Keep it safe along with planning consent forms as you'll need them when you come to sell.

How to decorate and furnish

The key thing to remember is that you aren't going to live there, your tenants are! You must avoid overspending and take care to buy things that are hard-wearing, easily cleaned, functional and long-lasting. Try to give the impression of a light, bright, spacious and airy property with a minimum of clutter. This can be done by using light curtains, mirrors, wall and table lights, plants and candles.

To add a bit of "wow" factor, it's also worth putting in a few other things too when trying to let (or sell) a property! If you don't want them there when the tenants move in, you can always store them. You are selling a lifestyle and your job is to help people visualise that lifestyle within your property. After all, that's just what developers do with show homes!

Even if you are advertising a property as "unfurnished", when doing a viewing have just enough stuff to make the place look homely. This would require beds in place (and made up), sofas and chairs. Here are some tips.

Curtains should be machine washable but alternatively consider using light roller blinds and Hessian or muslin fabrics. Curtain poles can also look good and aren't too expensive. For some reason, tenants are very good at breaking curtain tracks so always put in high quality curtain tracking. Make windows look wider by extending the track well beyond the frame on both sides.

Mirrors can be used to reflect light and give the impression of more space. If your ceiling is low, pictures can be used to attract the eye away from it. However, don't put too many pictures in or it will make a room feel small.

Lighting is useful for creating the right look. In sitting rooms and bedrooms standard lamps, table lamps and down lights are better than overheads at creating a softer feel while spotlights are best in kitchens. Candles, burning oils, fresh flowers, soft music, a nice rug, a laid table and fresh coffee brewing won't do your chances of letting any harm.

For carpets, use colours and designs that are light but which won't show every mark. A beige colour carpet with darker flecks is good for this. Have a large doormat, preferably a fitted one, put in. An alternative to carpeting is to use hardwood or laminate flooring with a few soft rugs thrown in to create a sense of warmth. However, wooden floors need sanding every three years and laminates aren't particularly hard-wearing. Also, if you're letting a flat, check that wooden or laminate floors are allowed under the lease and don't put them in if they will create a lot of noise for the flat downstairs. In the bathroom, ceramic tiles and linoleum are more water-resistant, hygienic and hardwearing than hardwood flooring or carpets.

Novice landlords are often tempted to overspend in the kitchen and bathroom. Keep it simple. Use stainless steel sinks with a tiled splashback to prevent walls getting grubby and mouldy. Roller blinds are better than slatted blinds which tend to get greasy and are hard to clean. When kitchen units get tatty, use new doors rather than buying a whole unit. Put a few classy cooking bottles in the kitchen to spell good cooking!

In the bathroom, light coloured suites are best and, again, make sure there are tiled splashbacks. Reduce condensation by having an extractor fan fitted and avoid wallpaper, which will peel if the room is not aired properly. Use gloss paints in the bathroom as these are more waterproof or use lots of tiling as it looks good and is easy to clean. Large tiles can quickly cover a large area. Break up tiles with a border tile half way up the wall and, again, use mirrors to increase the sense of space. Bathroom wall lights add a nice effect but will have to be properly enclosed. Tiles should be regrouted every two years and both bath and tiles should be properly sealed to avoid leaks.

Showers are one of the main causes of landlord call outs, because they leak. Unfortunately, tenants, especially foreign ones, like them. Get a good quality hard-wearing power shower and hope for the best. Change shower curtains after every let as they get grubby quickly and, if you can, install a glass screen, but make sure it stops all the water escaping! Toilets should be low level with a wooden loo seat. Finally, add some style to your bath and shower rooms with some quality shampoo bottles in the bathroom and put in some matching towels.

If you have more than one property try to stick to the same paint colour and sitting room suites in all of them. Touching up the colours in any one property can then be done with the same paint. Stick to neutral colours and remember that vinyl silk is easier to wash down than emulsion.

Don't forget the outside too. Remember, the first thing to do is to get people inside by making the property look nice from outside! Letting and estate agents call this "kerb appeal". Consider having some hanging baskets outside, repaint the front door, polish up brass fittings and letter-boxes and tidy the front garden. Keep unsightly dustbins out of sight. If the outside street is a mass of grafitti and abandoned cars, get onto the local authority to clean it up!

Gardens should be low maintenance because most tenants aren't interested in looking after plants and weeding. So no fast-growing hedges and bushes! Leave

tools to maintain gardens and include garden maintenance as a condition in your tenancy contract but don't
expect tenants to do much more than tidying it up just
before they move out. When showing a property in the
summer it's worth having a small fold away table, a few
chairs and even a parasol in the garden. It will help build
that lifestyle picture! Provide a washing line so tenants can
dry clothes outside, thus reducing condensation.

What you put into the property by way of other
furnishings will depend on your target market. Some
tenants will prefer you to supply white goods (e.g. fridge-
freezer, washing machine and cooker), some will also
expect to see beds, sofas, wardrobes and chests of drawers,
and others will prefer everything right down to kitchen
utensils, a TV and video. In the old days, whether or not
you furnished the property affected how easy it was to
repossess it at the end of the tenancy but this rule no
longer applies. How you furnish it, indeed whether you
furnish it at all, depends simply upon the type of tenant
you want to attract. Before you buy, put out a test advert
and, when tenants ring, ask them what furnishings they
would expect. That way when you've actually got the
property, you can furnish it to exactly the right level.

With my properties, I usually provide just basic white
goods plus sofas, chairs, beds and tables. However, if I
think the tenant is going to be good, pay a high rent and
stay for a long time, I'll include other things too. If tenants
are scarce, I'm more inclined to be flexible and meet their
requirements as there isn't any sense in a good tenant
walking away for the want of a wardrobe! However, I try
to avoid providing too much stuff, because it all needs to
be maintained and insured and, if the next tenant doesn't
want it, you then have to store it.

Doing viewings on a property that is already let

As soon as an existing tenant gives notice to leave, you should be planning viewings for new prospective tenants, so include a clause in your tenancy contract that allows you to conduct viewings with prospective tenants in the last month of the tenancy. This will help prevent void periods.

Unfortunately, you can't insist that the old tenants keep the place in a tidy and clean condition whilst they live there. However, I've had many tenants, who were so tidy and had such good taste, the property looked better with all their stuff in it than when they had left. When it's like this, it's easy to re-let it. If you get on well with your old tenants, they won't mind you bringing along little tricks like fresh flowers and bottles of balsamic vinegar to help re-let it!

Also, some tenants live in a mess and this is a problem when you need to do viewings with prospective tenants. Piles of clothes everywhere and yesterday's pizza lying on the floor won't impress anybody or help them visualise what it could be like. If your existing tenants are like this, there isn't really much you can do – you can't withhold part of their deposit (unless they fail to clean up when they leave). Try appealing to their better nature, get to the viewings very early to tidy up a bit or even offer them a cash incentive.

Where the place is really bad, then it's probably worth waiting until the existing tenants have gone before remarketing it. You can then go in and make it look good! Finally, don't forget always to notify existing tenants of times when you'll be doing viewings. Don't turn up unannounced!

Fully furnished lets where everything from china to cable and satellite TV are provided tend to be more the norm in up-market properties rented to top executives, often on short-term contracts. In some of these cleaning and laundry may need to be provided too. These types of lets are often more like "serviced apartments" and need to compete with hotels in terms of standard of furnishings and décor.

Remember, providing lots of furnishing means more cost and work. You'll need more contents insurance and a higher deposit too because the more there is, the more that can be damaged! The more mechanical and electrical items provided, the more that can break down too adding to costs in terms of time and money spent fixing or replacing them.

All furniture should comply with the soft furnishing regulations (see below). If you provide beds, don't buy cheap ones because tenants will soon complain that they are uncomfortable. Ideally, buy quality beds with storage space underneath (although if your tenant is a Feng Shui fan he won't store anything under the bed – bad vibes apparently). Avoid putting in furniture that's too big for the room as it will make the room feel small. Furniture should be in darker colours to avoid showing up every mark. Washable loose covers should be used on soft furnishings. Finally, never leave anything of sentimental value.

Legal regulations: Furnishing, gas safety, electrical, EPCs, HMOs and disability

There are a number of specific legal regulations that affect properties that are let out.

Soft furnishings

All soft furnishings must comply with the Furniture and Furnishings (Fire) (Safety) Regulations 1988 which say they must be fire safety compliant. Things that must comply are beds (including headboards and mattresses), sofas, garden furniture which could be used internally, cushions, pillows, loose and stretch covers for furniture. Look for the fire safety label stating it meets the requirements of the 1988 Safety Regulations. Things that are exempt are bed linen, loose covers for mattresses, pillow cases, curtains and carpets or furniture made before 1950.

Gas
The Gas Safety (Installation and Use) Regulations 1998 say landlords must ensure that gas appliances, fittings and flues provided for tenants' use are safe. Installation, maintenance and annual safety checks must be carried out by a Gas Safe Registered Installer for each gas appliance/ flue. Provided that everything is OK, the engineer will give you a CP12 Landlord's Gas Safety Certificate showing that everything is satisfactory. You have to give a copy to your tenant when any letting starts and have a new check done each year. Keep a copy for yourself. For additional safety, get a carbon monoxide detector fitted.

Before allowing anyone to do any work on gas in your property, ask to see his Gas Safe Registered Installer identification (ID) card. The Institute of Plumbing and Heating Engineering (IPHE) and the Association of Plumbing and Heating Contractors (see Appendix 2) have lists of Gas Safe Registered Installers.

Electrical
Whilst there is no legal requirement to have annual safety checks on electrical equipment, it's a criminal offence to "fail to ensure that the electrical system and appliances are

safe". (Electrical Equipment Safety Regulations 1994.) So it's wise to have electrical equipment and wiring checked before the first letting starts and have periodic checks done by a qualified electrician. Use an NICEIC-registered electrician or one from the Electrical Contractors Association (ECA), see Appendix 2, and keep a record of all safety checks.

All appliances have to be in working order and operating instructions and safety warning notices supplied. Particular attention should be paid to second-hand equipment, so always have these checked. In properties built after June 1992 and in houses classified as licensable HMOs (see below), there must be mains-wired smoke detectors on each floor. All HMOs should also have a full electrical safety check done at least every five years.

Any significant electrical work (for example, installing an electric shower or kitchen appliance) must be carried out by a 'competent' person.

Energy Performance Certificates (EPCs)
All tenants must be given a copy of the Energy Performance Certificate for the property. These cost about £50 per property, last for ten years and show how energy efficient the property is. You can use the one you were given when you bought the property, though if you have improved energy efficiency since you bought it, getting a new one done should pay off as it will show a better score for energy efficiency.

Licensing and Houses in Multiple Occupation (HMOs)
In broad terms, where three or more people occupy a property but don't form a single household, usually because they are not related, the property is classified by

the Government as a "House in Multiple Occupation" or HMO. The definition of HMO applies whether there is one or multiple tenancy agreements within the one property. An HMO can be a flat or a house.

In England and Wales, landlords with HMOs of three storeys or above *and* with five or more tenants have to get a licence. HMO licences impose tough management standards (and hence higher costs) to ensure that properties comply with fire and electrical safety standards and are not occupied by too many people; even the kind of person who can be a landlord for such a property is regulated.

For smaller HMOs the management standards amount to little more than what landlords should be doing anyway, with the main additional requirement being to have an electrical inspection carried out every five years.

However, it's potentially much tougher on licensable HMOs because of new onerous rules relating to the number of washbasins. These say that for licensable HMOs, where there are five or more occupiers, there must be one separate toilet (which should also have a hand washbasin) and at least one separate bathroom for every five occupiers. Also, if there are five or more occupiers, the local authority can require that each "unit of living accommodation" also has a washbasin or sink.

The killer requirement is, of course, the one requiring a separate hand washbasin in each bedroom. Many think this rule was just a little over the top and fortunately it looks like most local authorities are not imposing this regulation in their areas.

Any licensable HMO will also have to be inspected for health and safety hazards under the new Housing Health and Safety Rating System (HHSRS) within five years of an HMO licence being granted.

It's worth noting that local authorities can "extend" licensing in their area (or part of it) to HMOs with fewer than three levels or five tenants if they think there is a need. And if there is a local problem with anti-social behaviour or low housing demand, then ALL let properties can be licensed. To find out if your HMO may be in an area where extended licensing is being applied or is under consideration, check with your council's Environmental Health Officer or the Private Housing Department.

Fees for a licence vary greatly from around £50 in some local authorities up to £1,500 in others. Penalties for not getting a licence are severe – fines of up to £20,000 can be applied for landlords who don't register.

In Scotland and Northern Ireland *all* HMOs have to be licensed – i.e. mandatory licensing is not restricted to just those HMOs with three or more levels and five or more tenants; it applies to all HMOs.

In Scotland landlords of properties that are not HMOs must also be registered in a separate scheme. The minimum fee is £55 and there are additional fees for each local authority where you have a property and for each property that is let there is a charge of £11.

The Scottish registration scheme costs millions of pounds to administer and yet has seen only a handful of rogue landlords brought to justice. Fortunately, a proposal for a national register for England and Wales has been dropped (for now).

Some landlords have found that lenders are not comfortable with HMOs and restrict loan amounts or will only grant mortgages for HMOs to more experienced landlords. There are also reports that some landlords of licensable HMOs – faced with increasing costs of compliance – have sold up. However, other more experienced landlords sometimes like the potentially higher rents that HMOs can bring and actively seek out HMO properties, especially where there is a large student population combined with a lack of college or other purpose-built student accommodation.

Conversion of a property to and from HMO status may require planning permission – this varies by council and size of HMO so check with your local authority.

Disability

The law defines disability as any mental or physical impediment that adversely affects someone's ability to carry out normal day to day activities. The disability has to be "long term", which means it has to be expected to last for over a year. Things like cancer, HIV and multiple sclerosis are included within this definition.

Landlords should make "reasonable adjustments" to their property if asked unless they have "reasonable grounds" for refusing. The reasonableness test involves questioning if any change is really going to help the disabled person, and disruption to others has to be taken into account too.

So, whilst you might be expected to provide a large print tenancy agreement for the partially sighted person, amend a parking policy to allow for an essential motor vehicle or allow a guide dog; you would not need to change or alter any physical feature which is a part of the design or construction of the building.

Failure to comply with the rules could in the worst case lead to court proceedings, claims for damages and if the property is an HMO, the loss of an HMO licence.

Minor adaptations costing less than £1,000 may be

provided freely by the local housing department in England and grants from other bodies and charities may also be available.

How to get the right insurance cover

Obviously, before taking ownership of a property, the buildings must be insured. If you're getting a mortgage, your lender will insist that this is in place, will ask to see proof of the policy and be noted as an "interested party". For flats, the insurance will normally be arranged by the freeholder.

The more specialist buy-to-let mortgage companies and most landlords' associations have specialist buildings' insurance policies for landlords. Other sources are letting agents and commercial insurance brokers. Typically, the policies include a small amount of contents cover which is good if you're only providing a limited amount of furnishings and don't need a separate contents policy. Cover for loss of rent, temporary accommodation and storage of furniture following fire or water damage should be provided too.

Most specialist landlord policies will include cover for public and employer's liability up to at least five million pounds. Even if you just pay a friend to do a job for you, he will become an employee in law! Also useful is a 24–7 emergency assistance feature, especially one which covers the cost of a call out to deal with an emergency. These are really worth getting because the insurer will send out its emergency tradesmen to do an initial fix, with the cost covered up to a certain amount. This will save you having to buy a separate emergency cover policy which is usually expensive for what it is! If your insurance has emergency assistance, ask about service standards because, if you have a flood, you want the problem dealt with the same day, not next week!

Check the policy exclusions. Some policies won't cover students, people on housing benefit, asylum seekers, short-term lets or properties let to social landlords such as housing associations or local councils. Most won't cover properties that are unoccupied for more than three weeks unless the insurer is informed in advance and regular visits to the property are carried out. Others will insist the property is let on an assured shorthold tenancy. Where the insurance company perceives that the risk is higher, it may cover it, but charge a higher premium.

Malicious damage by tenants rarely happens but it's often not covered, even under special landlords' policies. So even if you end up hating your tenants, don't do anything that may lead them to trash the property!

If you're a nervous first-time landlord with a big mortgage, it might be worth considering a rent guarantee policy which will pay your rent if the tenant defaults. Typically they cost about 3 to 6 per cent of the rent (though some letting agents may include it "free" within their fee for finding a tenant). Typically these policies pay rent for between six and twelve months, although they often don't kick in until two months' rent has been missed. If you buy one, look for one that also covers legal expenses to evict the tenant.

I don't buy this type of cover as a stand-alone policy because I'm confident my vetting procedure will weed out tenants who can't or won't pay. I've also found that, to qualify, the tenant has to score so highly on the insurance company's own credit scoring system, that the chances of his defaulting would be very low anyway! However, I'll admit they do give useful peace of mind (at a cost!).

The level of excess (or deductible) on a specialist

landlord policy varies from about £100 to £250 for normal claims though it's normally £1,000 for subsidence claims. Block buildings policies that apply on flats tend to have standard excesses from £250 to £500 and no contents cover at all, so your carpets and curtains will be at risk if you don't have separate cover. Block polices will also generally not have any liability cover protecting you as the flat owner and landlord.

Tell your tenants that you aren't responsible for any accidental damage they do, nor for damage to their own possessions whatever the cause. I always advise my tenants to take out cover for their own possessions, and to ensure that it includes accidental damage cover too.

If you're letting what used to be your own home, your current cover will not be suitable. Most domestic insurance policies do not cover rented property at all so if the property used to be your home, tell your insurers that the property is being let and check if they can provide a suitable specialist landlord policy.

Recent big flood events have pushed up the cost of insurance especially in flood risk areas and there is now a real risk that insurers may withdraw cover completely in areas where flood defences have not been adequately maintained by the Government. Check whether you are at risk at the Environment Agency website – see Appendix 2.

Good advice for when you make an insurance claim
Most policies won't pay for replacement taps, toilets or boilers, though they usually pay for "trace and access" to find the source of a leak. So tell your plumber or boiler repairer to include "trace and access" on his invoice if he's doing a trace, repair and replacement job.

Keeping everyone informed:
Telling people who "need to know"

Being a landlord involves quite a lot of administration. Apart from ensuring that gas, electricity and furnishings are safe and that insurance is in place, you'll need to keep the council tax and utilities people informed too. As soon as you take ownership, take meter readings for electricity, gas and water. If you hope to let quickly, it's probably only necessary to contact them once the property has been let so you can tell them the opening and closing meter readings and the names of the new tenants in one go. If it's likely to be some time until your first let, for example if you are having work done, then give the meter readings straightaway.

Don't forget that if the property is furnished you may have to pay council tax until the property is let, when it becomes the responsibility of the tenant. For short-term lettings it may be simpler to keep utility bills and council tax in your name. It's worth knowing which utility companies are cheapest and, if you aren't likely to be using too much energy, choose a supplier that doesn't make a daily standing charge.

If you have a flat that will be let out you must tell the freeholder and/or his managing agent. Some blocks don't allow short lets of, say, less than six months so check the terms of your lease first. Also, watch out for local council regulations because some stipulate that all lets should be for more than three months' duration.

If the property used to be your home and you have permission to let it out, tell the mortgage and insurance company. Remember to advise everyone who "needs to know" of your correspondence address and always to keep a record of who you spoke to and when.

To avoid the risk of being a victim of identity fraud, ensure that all bills are sent to a secure correspondence address.

6

HOW TO GET THE TENANCY AGREEMENT CORRECT

Before your first let starts, there are two important bits of documentation you should prepare for your tenant. These are the tenancy agreement and something I call the "House Guide" for the property, which is basically a guide to the property including a list of dos and don'ts and setting out what should be done in an emergency.

For normal lettings, whilst you don't strictly need a written agreement, it's best to set down what the tenant can and can't do. It's also harder to evict a tenant if there is no written agreement. If you are letting a room in your own home to lodgers or doing holiday lettings you don't need a formal agreement, but you should still keep relevant paperwork to prove the terms of the letting, if only in the event of a dispute.

The different types of tenancy
Assured shorthold tenancies (AST)
The main form of tenancy used today is called the Assured Shorthold Tenancy (AST) or Short Assured

Tenancy in Scotland. I've included in Appendix 1 a copy of the AST that I use. With an AST, the tenant has the right to occupy the property exclusively and the landlord can charge a market rent.

For tenancies starting after 28 February 1997, provided that you don't live there, it is not a holiday let, the rent is under £100,000 and it is not let to a company, then the tenancy will be an AST unless you state otherwise. The great attraction of an AST is that you can always recover the property at the end of the fixed term, provided that proper notice of at least two months has been given to the tenant.

If your tenancy started after 15 January 1989 but before the end of February 1997, it would be either an Assured Tenancy (AT) or an Assured Shorthold Tenancy (AST), unless you stated otherwise. The main difference between an AT and an AST is that with an AST you can always automatically get possession of the property at the end of the six-month term of the tenancy or later provided that you give at least two months' notice, whereas with an AT the only real way to end one would be for the tenant seriously to breach the terms of the tenancy. Also, only an AST has to be protected in a tenancy deposit scheme. (From January 1989 to February 1997, to create an AST, you had to serve a special notice, called a Section 20 notice, before the start of the tenancy. If you didn't it would automatically be an AT.)

Rent Act tenancies

Tenancies which started before 15 January 1989 are regulated by the Rent Act 1977 and are often called "Rent Act" tenancies. They aren't as good as ASTs and ATs because with Rent Act tenancies it's very difficult to evict and landlords can only charge a "fair rent". A fair rent is whatever a rent tribunal says is fair and tends to be somewhat below market rents! Also, once a fair rent is set, it usually can't be challenged for two years. And, no, before you ask, you can't convert a Rent Act tenancy to an AST! Finally, evicting a Rent Act tenant requires specialist legal advice.

With their disadvantages, these forms of tenancy are declining in number and only a masochist landlord would issue a Rent Act tenancy today! Properties sold at auction sometimes have sitting Rent Act tenants and this should be reflected in a lower house price.

Company tenancies and rents over £100,000 per year
Where the tenant is a company instead of an individual or the rent is over £100,000, the tenancy agreement may look the same as an AST with the main difference being that it's not bound by the six-month rule but by common law instead. Again, as with an AT, it doesn't need to be protected in a tenancy deposit scheme.

The benefits of company lets are that a company can't have security of tenure, payments are often made in advance for a period of three or six months and the company may be more secure than an individual. However, be wary if the tenant works for a foreign government because courts can't enforce breaches of contract if the person has diplomatic immunity. Also, if you let to a company you should check their financial position first.

Many company lets are of less than six months' duration and are popular with companies as they are cheaper than putting an executive in a hotel. Most executives prefer them to hotel living too! Rents should be 10 to 40 per cent above what's achievable on a longer term let but there may be more voids and frequent changes of tenant means more work finding new tenants, checking in and out and keeping the property in good repair. If the rent is high and the let short term, the client will reasonably expect higher standards.

Letting rooms in your own home (Licence to occupy)
If you let rooms in your home to lodgers, they have fewer rights and you can end the tenancy when you want and without ever needing to get a court order. A written agreement isn't essential but is useful to set out dos and don'ts anyway. A key thing is to specifically make clear you are not giving the lodger exclusive possession (i.e. landlord is excluded) of any part of your property including his own room.

Holiday lets
If the property is let for a few weeks for a holiday, you can evict the occupiers if they refuse to leave without getting a court order. A formal tenancy agreement isn't required but you should keep invoices and correspondence to prove the intention was to be a holiday let. For more on holiday lettings see pages 238 and 249.

The assured shorthold tenancy (AST) agreement: What's in it?

Since the most important form of agreement is the AST, it's worth saying some more about it.

Most ASTs are for a fixed term, normally six or twelve months. When the term comes to an end, if the landlord agrees, the tenant can stay on, with the same terms and conditions as before. The landlord can get the property back at the end of the fixed term or any time after that, provided that he gives two months' notice.

Where there is more than one tenant on the agreement, each person is "jointly and severally liable" for the full rent. So, if two people sign the same agreement to rent a house at £1,500 per month, if one leaves, the other will have to find the whole £1,500 himself. If he can't, you're entitled to sue either of them for the whole of the rent for any period it remains unpaid. It is important to make this clear to tenants, particularly to groups of friends renting a house together.

In practice, what happens is that the remaining person would get someone new in. However, it's important that anyone new is properly reference-checked and a new agreement issued with both persons' names on it. Again, you should make it clear that they are each jointly and severally liable for the whole rent, not just one half of it. If the old tenant and the new tenant didn't know each other beforehand, this is quite a commitment for them to take on as they need to trust not only you, but each other too!

If you aren't certain that someone can pay his rent, it's worth getting a guarantor who can pay if the tenant defaults. The guarantor will need to be referenced too. (For more on referencing see Chapter 7.) The guarantee can be simply tacked on at the end of the agreement and signed by the guarantor with the signature witnessed by a third party when the letting commences. It needs to confirm he will pay if the tenant defaults or breaches the tenancy agreement in any way resulting in cost to the landlord. Alternatively, the guarantor can sign a separate letter of guarantee.

The agreement shouldn't contain any clauses that are unfair or which reduce the rights of the tenants as consumers. This doesn't mean the rent has to be "fair", it just means that individual contract terms can't be unreasonable. An example of an unfair term would be one saying that the landlord had the right to come and view the property at any time without giving prior notice. An unfair term wouldn't invalidate the whole agreement – it would just make the unfair clause unenforceable.

The effect of the fixed term is that you can't evict a tenant within that term unless he has breached the terms of the agreement. It also means that if a tenant moves out after, say, three months of a fixed six-month tenancy, you could try to claim rent for a further three months (but only if you hadn't let it to someone else after he'd left). In practice though, you must be flexible. If the tenant had always paid rent on time, but had to leave early due to difficult circumstances, but found a suitable replacement tenant, then you must be accommodating. After all, if the old tenant hasn't got a job, then it's going to be hard for him to pay the rent anyway!

If the old tenant can't find a replacement, I'd let him go with six weeks' notice, during which time I'd be fairly confident I'd find a new tenant. In return, however, I'd make it clear that the property should be left in a pristine condition whenever any prospective tenant came to view. I'd also insist that the property was immaculately clean when he came to leave!

The fixed term can be longer than six months. However, I'd avoid making it too long because if, say the tenants kept annoying neighbours or continually paid the rent late, then you'd want to be rid of them earlier. If you've arranged a twelve-month tenancy, you may end up waiting twelve months to be rid of them. With a six-month term, you can serve notice at the beginning requiring possession at the end of the six-month term. This saves having to remember to serve the notice during the tenancy and means that the tenant knows the position right from the start. For more on giving notice and getting possession, see Chapters 8 and 9.

A six-month term is also good if you use a letting agent because some agents still take their commission upfront, based on the period of the contract. So the longer the fixed term, the more you have to pay the agent upfront. For example, if the letting agent charges 10 per cent for finding a tenant for a twelve-month term at £1,000 per month, his commission will be £1,200, i.e. 10 per cent x 12 months x £1,000. However, on a six-month contract the commission would be only £600. Unsurprisingly, most agents try to get you to agree a twelve-month tenancy.

The agreement will describe the property to be rented, the start date of the agreement and the names of the landlord and tenants. It should make it clear if any part of the property is excluded, such as garages or outbuildings. It will specify the rental amount and should say that it's to be paid in advance and to a specified account. Normally, the rent should be paid monthly. If you opt for weekly payments you should provide a rent book.

Normally utilities (including council tax) will be paid by the tenants but you can pay these if you wish, especially if it's a short-term let or an HMO. The agreement must say who is going to pay these bills.

The amount of the deposit will be stated and mention as to what it will be used for and whether any interest will be paid on it. Most tenants don't expect to receive interest, but it's worth stating so anyway. I normally charge a deposit of about five to six weeks' rent but, if you supply a lot of furnishings, ask for up to seven weeks' rent. Deposits should be less than two months' rent as this could give tenants a right to sub-let.

Make two original copies of the agreement. You and your

tenants (and the guarantor if applicable) sign both copies on the day they move in after they have paid the balance of the deposit and the first month's rent and before they move in any of their own stuff. Ideally, everyone should initial each page. Each party keeps one copy.

All new ASTs issued in England and Wales from 6 April 2007 where a deposit is taken must have the deposit protected under a tenancy deposit scheme. You should state on the agreement which of the various schemes it is protected in. See Chapter 8, page 193.

A sample of the AST agreement I use is shown in Appendix 1, on page 263.

What tenants need to know:
The emergency and maintenance "House Guide"
It's very important to give tenants some guidance to help them look after your property properly. In particular, those who haven't rented before will need to be told what to do in the event of an emergency and how to deal with routine maintenance. Explain to tenants that they are responsible for minor repairs like changing fuses and bulbs as well as taking prompt action and seeking help if anything more serious happens.

Here's a typical scenario. It's 9 pm on Christmas Eve and the phone rings. It's one of your tenants and he's calling to tell you that water is pouring out of a pipe and flooding the hallway, the neighbours in the flat below are going crazy and he doesn't know what to do. This has been going on for three hours, but he's only just managed to find your phone number!

This is the kind of problem many landlords face from time to time and, for some reason, they have a knack of happening at the most awkward times, usually on public holidays, at weekends or late at night. It's a pain because it ruins your weekend; you either have to go and deal with it yourself or pay someone, just when charge-out rates are most expensive. So, how can landlords plan for such events and what should they do when they happen?

The first thing is to make your tenants aware of what to do and who to contact in an emergency. New tenants should be told it's their contractual duty to act promptly to report anything that could damage the property or give rise to a claim. You could add that if they fail to do so they could be held liable for the resulting cost!

Give your tenants a written set of instructions (a "House Guide") to follow so they know what action to take to protect themselves, the property (and in the case of flats) surrounding properties too. Ideally, the House Guide should cover what to do in the event of a problem with plumbing, drains, gas or electricity and is invaluable because a delay of only half an hour in getting a problem fixed can cost thousands in damage.

Get tenants to look out for problems

Many tenants ignore minor problems until they become serious or affect them directly. A friend of mine had a tenant who ignored the fact that water was flowing from the toilet overflow pipe outside his flat. As the water flowed out from the pipe it cascaded down onto the wall of the flat below where it eventually seeped into the wall and caused damage to the internal decoration. An angry neighbour and a big claim could have been avoided if the tenant had taken action to stop the overflow earlier.

Every time you let your property, talk through the House Guide with your tenants and leave a laminated copy on a notice board, where they can find it quickly when they need to. Show them where the mains fuse board is, how to turn the gas off at the mains, where the water stop valve is and how to work the heating, washing machine, etc, using the operating manuals.

As well as dealing with emergencies, the House Guide should highlight some basics for tenants to look out for. In particular, overflowing pipes, damp smells, flaking wallpaper and short-circuiting fuses are things that indicate the presence of hidden problems that need fixing.

Damage caused by water leaks can be very expensive if the problem isn't fixed quickly. The most common causes are boilers, pumps, dripping taps, leaking pipes, toilet overflows and showers. Usually, the cost of things damaged by water is covered under insurance, provided that you (or your tenant) weren't negligent or slow in dealing with the problem. It's worth remembering that, in extreme cases, insurance companies can limit what they'll pay out, or even refuse the claim altogether, if they think you (or your tenants) had been careless or failed to take prompt action to reduce damage.

Extra special care and responsibility is required for flats above another property because in the worst case you could be held liable by a neighbour (or his insurance company) if water escaping from your property causes damage to his furnishings or fittings. This could include the cost of replacing curtains, carpets and furnishings, repairing ceilings, repainting, cost of temporary accommodation, damages for inconvenience and even the cost of a court case! It can all add up, especially if your neighbour happens to be a lawyer!

The House Guide should contain the following instructions:

- In the event of a gas leak, windows and doors should be opened. No one should smoke, use naked flames or touch electrical devices. The gas supply should be turned off by pulling downwards on the gas lever and Transco's twenty-four-hour emergency line (0800 111 999) called.
- In the event of a problem with the mains drain, the water company should be called. (Include their number.)
- In the event of a water leak, the water should be turned off at the stop valve. (Say where the valve is.)
- If the property is going to be empty overnight or for more than twelve hours when the weather is cold, leave enough heating on to prevent the freezing of the water system.
- Air rooms, especially bathrooms to stop the build up of condensation.
- Regularly check that no water is running from overflows or pipes.
- Look out for damp smells and flaking walls.
- Regularly check that the washing machine remains securely plumbed in.
- Do not allow the washing machine or dishwasher to operate when no one is in.
- Ensure that the shower curtain is pulled across during use.
- Avoid fat, food, tampons, nappies, hair or other obstructions being put down toilets or sinks.

The Guide should contain information on how to relight the boiler, where the stop valve (stop cock) is and how to open and close it. A good tip here is that, when opening the valve, it should always be turned back half a turn from the fully open position to avoid the valve sticking.

Relevant telephone numbers for you, your preferred tradesmen (and your insurance company's emergency assistance number, if covered for emergency call outs) should be put in the House Guide, so tenants can contact them directly in an emergency. It's also worth including the phone number for the local water and electricity suppliers.

The House Guide should show the location of the mains fuse box and isolator switch and how to replace mains fuses and smoke detector batteries. Where you have battery-operated smoke detectors, your tenant must be able to get to them easily to replace old batteries.

You could also include in the House Guide useful information like the refuse collection day, details of local doctors and pharmacies, good restaurants and the location of the nearest trains, tubes, trams and buses.

Water damage in blocks of flats is a real headache for flat owners and is one reason why buildings insurance in blocks (especially those in which most flats are let out) can be so high.

So, if you have a flat which is below another flat, it's worthwhile getting to know the people who live upstairs. Ask them what they would do in the event of, say, a water leak. Do they know how to turn off the gas or water? If the property is let out, I can almost guarantee that their landlord or his agent has left them no instructions at all. In fact, it never ceases to amaze me that some landlords are prepared to spend a lot of money on a flat, only to risk it being badly damaged for the want of a few simple instructions! Do yourself a favour and give them a copy of your House Guide. (If their flat is in the same layout as yours, the stop valve and gas shut off valve will probably be in the same location.)

7

HOW TO FIND A GOOD TENANT

So, you've got the property, it meets all the legal regulations and your tenancy agreement is ready. Now you need to find a tenant.

How do you go about finding a good one? There are various options. You could get friends in, use a housing association, a letting agent or find a tenant yourself. This chapter tells you everything you need to know – where to advertise, what to say and how to check potential tenants out. If you use a letting agency, this chapter will tell you how to choose a good one and get them to work effectively for you.

A word of warning! Even if you use a letting agent, you are strongly advised to read the whole of this chapter, especially the parts about referencing tenants because, if your agent gets this wrong and you get a bad tenant, it will cost you (not your agent) a small fortune. This means you *must* make sure that your agent has checked out your potential tenant properly!

This is a long chapter and I make no apologies for that

because getting a good tenant is absolutely critical for success as a landlord.

Letting to friends . . . and why you shouldn't!

You may be tempted to let to friends or relations especially if you have some friends who just happen to be looking for a property to rent. After all, you won't need to worry about advertising, and, if they can move in right away, there won't be any periods when your property is vacant and bringing in no rental income. And, of course, your friends will move out when you want them to. Well, that's what you hope.

Letting to friends sounds very good but I'd advise against it. They say you should never mix business with pleasure and nowhere is this truer than in the lettings business. Your friends will not like the fact that you have power over them and will probably not see the relationship as a commercial one. So, if you want to charge a deposit or put the rent up, you will find it hard to do this with friends and they won't like you for doing it either. So, if you want to keep your friends as friends don't let to them in the first place.

Getting your existing tenants to find new tenants

If you are already letting the property to tenants you like, but they have to move on, why not ask them to help find your new tenants? They presumably have friends who may have been to the property and liked it and they will know you are a good landlord.

Letting to a social housing organisation

Letting to a social landlord is becoming increasingly popular at the lower end of the market. Many local authorities and housing associations can take on your property for a long term (typically between two and four years). They will pay you a rent which is just below market rent and they will frequently look after some of the maintenance for you. They will then sublet to their own tenants. Your contract is with the local council or housing association not the tenant and rent is therefore guaranteed. The only real drawback is that you have no control over whom they let it out to, which could be a real issue for you if your neighbours are the type who are active complainers. These types of let are sometimes called Private Sector Leasing Schemes (PSLS) or Housing Association Leasing Schemes (HALS).

In many ways this is better than letting directly to people who are on housing benefit. With a PSLS, your rent is guaranteed and there is no void nor any chance of tenant default nor of the council clawing back from you money they paid direct to you but which turned out to be based on false information provided by the tenant. Also, you don't have to worry about re-letting the property and finding new tenants for a few years and there is no agency fee to pay. Check with the council or look under Housing Associations in your phone book or on your Internet search engine.

Using a letting agent

Another way to find tenants is to use the services of a letting agent.

There are of course many times when you have to use a letting agent. For example, if you don't live close to the property it would be impractical to do it any other way. The other reason is if you simply don't have the time or inclination to do it yourself. After all, why waste time advertising and interviewing tenants if your friendly local agent will do it for you anyway at a fraction of the cost of your own lost work or leisure time?

So, if you live far away, are a high earner in your day job and/or you are just too busy, then a letting agent may be good for you.

Now, as with anything, there are some agents who are good and some who are poor. In my experience the majority of agents are pretty good but you can often do a better job yourself. I shall discuss how you do it yourself in a moment. But first, a quick look at what a letting agent actually does.

A letting agency can either just be involved in finding a tenant or it can be involved additionally with managing a tenancy. In this chapter, we shall just concern ourselves with their role of finding a tenant. (See Chapter 8 for advice on managing a tenancy.)

Typically the fee a letting agency will charge to *smaller* landlords (i.e. with fewer than, say, three properties) for finding a tenant is between 7 and 10 per cent + VAT of the rental income for the term of the agreement. For this they will find a tenant for you, collect the first month's rent and deposit and set up the tenancy agreement. So, if the rent is £1,000 a month for six months, they will charge as follows: £1,000 x 6 x 10% + 20% = £720.

For short-term lets, although rents will be higher, the agency's finding and management fees will be in the range from 20 per cent to 40 per cent.

Many letting agents – especially outside London – will charge about four weeks' rent rather than a percentage based fee.

Look at any letting agency's advertising material and it should be full of the benefits of using them. (If it isn't full of such claims, then you should be very worried – after all, if they can't market their own company, how are they going to market your property!) Some of the ancillary benefits they claim for using their services are listed below. However, as you will see from reading about each of these services, their expertise can be acquired easily yourself.

Letting agents prepare a tenancy agreement in accordance with current legislation
Any agent can prepare a tenancy agreement in accordance with current legislation. However, you can easily obtain an up-to-date standard tenancy agreement in any bookshop and many books on the subject (including this one) will have a standard draft agreement with all the main terms and conditions. Alternatively, if you join a landlords' organisation, such as the National Landlords or Residential Landlords Associations, they should also be able to provide you with an agreement. Once you have your standard agreement, you then need to keep up-to-date with any changes in legislation and amend it accordingly.

Keep up-to-date
Keep up-to-date with legislation by joining a landlords' association.

Letting agents can value your property and advise you what rent can be achieved
An agent will happily value your property and advise you what rent can be achieved. However, you can get a rough idea of what's achievable by looking in letting agents' windows, on the Internet at sites like Rightmove or in the local paper.

Moreover, if you bought a property with the intention of letting it out, you really should have worked out what the likely rent is before you bought it! For more on estimating achievable rent see Chapters 2 and 3. (By the way, if you bought from a developer you should never trust the developer or an agent linked to him to give you an honest assessment of the achievable rent.)

Letting agents can advise you about decorating, furnishing and the laws on electrical and gas safety, HMOs and disability
True they can do this. Alternatively, everything you need to know is in Chapter 5 of this book.

Letting agents can do a detailed inventory
An agent can do the check-ins and check-outs, read the meters and arrange an inventory or appoint an independent clerk to do this. There will be an extra charge for handling the inventory. However, if you want to appoint an independent inventory clerk to record the condition of the property and the fixtures and fittings, you could appoint one yourself – possibly at less cost. Never skimp on doing a thorough inventory at check-in and check-out and ideally have an independent inventory clerk do it for you – much the best option in case of disputes later.

Letting agents have a shop or an Internet site that will attract tenants
This is where agents really add value because lots of tenants now use Internet portals like RightMove to find property to rent and any decent agent should be with one or more of these portals. However, whilst an agent will attract people to their shop or Internet site, you can also

generate a lot of interest through your own advertising and it is also now possible to get on all the main letting portals via specialist landlord letting sites for a fee of about £50 to £60 per property.

Now, what are the drawbacks to using a letting agent?

Some letting agents have longer void periods
In my experience, properties which are marketed by letting agencies can sometimes suffer longer periods without tenants (the dreaded "void periods").

If you are letting through an agent and there is a long period when your property is between tenants, you can be sure that the agents aren't losing as much sleep as you are. After all it's not their money which is being lost on mortgage loan payments, service charges, etc, whilst no rent comes in!

The reason for the longer voids is that some agents are basically not very efficient. A poor agent will take longer to find a suitable tenant and take a lot longer to complete reference checks.

Some letting agents can be prone to exaggeration
Some of the less reputable agents are prone to exaggeration or even telling downright lies. Here is a typical scenario. You get a phone call from an agent who has seen the property that you are trying to let in a local paper. "Hello, Mr L, we saw your ad in *Loot*. We have twenty blue-chip tenants we can send round today for our usual commission."

Now, for some reason these blue-chip tenants never materialise. They either don't exist at all or, if they do, they tend not to be all that blue-chip! Yes, they might work in an investment bank, but as a cleaner, not a banker! If you get such a call from an agent, ask yourself this – if a letting agent was any good would he be wasting time scouring newspapers and cold calling landlords?

I have experienced agents saying that they have sent people round when they haven't. Try to catch them out – if the property is empty, leave some post right behind the door. If it hasn't moved when you next come round, they are obviously lying about having been to your property. If your existing tenants are still in the property ask them if the agent has really had as many people round to view as he claims.

Most decent agents don't get up to these kinds of tricks, but there are undoubtedly a few odd rogues that do.

Some letting agents are expensive and can hurt your cash flow
Agents can be expensive and hurt your cash flow. They generally charge you upfront, which means that the 10 per cent plus VAT of the six or twelve months' rental income will usually come out of the first month's rent – obviously bad for cash flow! If the tenant leaves early or doesn't pay, you are really stuffed – having paid the agent's fee in full but had no or little rent. So see if you can get the agent's fee paid in stages as the tenancy progresses and based only on a six-month term, even if the actual fixed term is longer. The agent won't like this suggestion, but may accept if you push hard enough! Tell him if he's confident that his tenant will stay the course then he has no need to worry.

Also, don't forget, some agents may try to charge repeat fees if tenants stay on at the end of the initial six-month term. So, unless you terminate the tenancy or have it specially written into the contract with the agent, you could be paying your agent forever. So, read the agent's contract with you carefully and amend anything you don't like. Try to get a sliding commission fee and get this written into your agreement.

Some letting agents still levy additional charges on the tenant. I often find tenants are charged fixed fees for processing their applications, completing reference checks and doing inventories that are way above the actual cost of these services. This will obviously put tenants off or make them feel that they have been ripped off. Not a good start to a landlord/tenant relationship!

Some letting agents aren't as thorough or as quick as you would be
Some agents aren't as thorough or as quick as you could be. Take the job of referencing tenants. I thoroughly vet all my tenants and I can do it in forty-eight hours. Letting agents tend to outsource this job which means it takes a lot longer than this. And I often wonder if those doing the referencing for the agent employ their sixth sense to sniff out a potentially troublesome tenant. If there was a nagging worry about a potential tenant would they reject him?

How to find a good letting agent
Assuming you are going to use a letting agent to advertise your property, how do you pick a good one? Obviously, the best recommendations are personal recommendations especially from someone who has done it – i.e. another landlord.

If you don't know another landlord, ask to speak to two or three of the agency's existing landlords. If they won't let you, go elsewhere.

If you are a member of a local landlords' association ask them if they can recommend any agents locally. Also, look in the local and free newspapers. Do they advertise in there? Gauge how much of their business is letting property as opposed to, say, selling houses.

Read their brochures – are they professionally written? I have seen lots which are full of spelling errors. Ask to meet the staff who will be handling your letting. How professional are they? Look at their office – if it's dirty and disorganised, they will be disorganised too and potential tenants will also have a poor impression.

Is their office in a good location where it will attract lots of potential tenants? Does it open on Saturdays? Do they have an answer phone to take messages for people who call "out of hours"? Do all their properties appear on all the big letting portals like Primelocation or RightMove? Do they let properties that are like yours or are all their properties more up-market (or down-market) than yours? Pick an agent in *your* market!

The letting agency should have a contract with you telling you how they will go about marketing your property and what you will pay them for doing this. Review this carefully and tell them if you want any item amended. Refuse any contract that requires you to give an agent sole agency on advertising your property for a set time period – you should be free to fire an incompetent agent any time you wish and find tenants yourself without paying commission to the agent.

If you happen to have used the agency as a tenant, you will have some useful experience of them. However, be wary. Just because they have been a good agency when you were a tenant doesn't mean they are good at the business of finding tenants. Also, be wary if your experience of them was from some time ago as there is a very quick turnover of staff at letting agents.

If an agent wants to take a non-returnable security deposit as part of a "finder's fee", then go somewhere else. Also, if all they are doing is finding a tenant, then they should not hold on to tenants' deposits – these should either be put in one of the tenancy deposit protection schemes, with the money held in a separate client account, or handed over to you for you to protect it in one of the recognised schemes. If the letting agent is protecting it, ask to see proof of all this as some agents have failed to do this, used the cash as working capital and then gone bust, leaving the landlord liable for the tenants' deposit.

You should ask whether the letting agent is a member of ARLA (the Association of Residential Letting Agents), the National Approved Letting Scheme (NALS), the RICS (Royal Institution of Chartered Surveyors), UKALA (UK Association of Letting Agents) or the NAEA (the National Association of Estate Agents). Some of these organisations have a code of conduct and a fidelity bonding scheme (client money protection) which means that if the agent goes out of business the landlord will lose money in suspension but not the tenants' deposit. Check what's available.

Ask the agency what references they ask for and insist on being able to see any they obtain. Also insist that you retain the right to accept or reject any tenant they find. (A word of caution here: don't forget to make it clear to the agent – preferably in writing – what sort of tenants you will accept and what sort you will reject. You don't want to waste the agent's time unnecessarily.)

Test the agency. Phone them up anonymously and

make an enquiry about exactly the type of property you are trying to let through them. How well did they market your property, if at all? Even better, you could get a friend to do the same thing and, this time, actually get him to go and view your property with the agent. Your friend will be able to tell you how well the agent marketed your property and how knowledgeable he was. Did your agent know his facts about your property? Although most agents are very clued up, there will be some who are incompetent or in complete ignorance of your property or of the local area. Don't forget to buy your friend a drink or a meal as thanks!

It must be said that some agents can get rents about 10 per cent higher than private landlords can achieve. As this is about the same as the fee that they charge for finding a tenant, it leaves the landlord no worse (or better off). However, very good agents can get higher rents still.

Lastly, don't ever ask a friend or relation to act as your "agent" and look for tenants for you. You might be tempted to do this if, say, you are away for a few weeks or if you are too mean to employ an agent. Believe me, your friend will screw it up much worse than the worst letting agent and not only will you have the tenant from hell already moved in, but the tenant will not have paid you a penny in rent and won't be about to move out soon. You may also ruin your friendship with your friend. So don't ever, ever do this! Letting property is not easy so if you don't have time to do it yourself, then employ a professional agent not a friend who is an amateur.

How to find a tenant yourself

There are three parts to finding a tenant yourself. Firstly, you need to advertise. Secondly, you need to pre-screen and reference check the respondents so that you can separate the wheat from the chaff and find your ideal tenant. Thirdly, you need to make all the final preparations for the tenant to move in.

Advertising your property is simple. It comes down to three things – where to advertise it, when to advertise it and what to say in your advert.

Where to advertise your property
Your first decision is where to advertise the property. To some extent, the type of property will determine the media (choice of publication, website). So if the property you have is somewhere posh then the publication or website you choose should be more up-market too.

Bear in mind though that some publications will cover a large range of properties and a lot of these are free to advertisers. *Gumtree. com* is a good example of a free publication with a strong London presence and a wide range of properties (though it is less strong on more up-market properties). Local papers are also good and advertising in the window of a busy local newsagent can bring a surprisingly good response.

If you are prepared to let to students, then universities, colleges and hospitals are good places to advertise. Keep in with the Accommodation Officer and time your advertising when students are looking (this varies by college but can be up to nine months before the end of the academic year)! If you are a member of a local or national landlord association, they may have a website where you can advertise for free. You could also advertise on your own work intranet site, if you have one. Consider also your local supermarket, corner shop, gym and library notice boards. Contact any large local employer in the area. However, by far the best way to advertise these days is online. You can get your advert on the main letting portals for about £50 to £60. Write some good copy and get some good photos taken.

When to advertise it
The second decision is when to advertise it. If your property is available for rent, you'll just have to market it, whatever time of year it is. However, it is still useful to know something of the seasonality of the rental market.

In most big urban centres, especially those with student populations, the lettings market goes a bit dead between June and early August and from mid November to Boxing Day. When the students go home, people go on holidays and businesses take breaks, the letting population inevitably falls. There is a pick-up in September and mid January due to returning students looking for accommodation and companies recruiting more staff.

So, if you already have a tenant in place who calls to give you notice, which would mean advertising for new tenants in the quiet months, do all you can to make him stay that little bit longer. Consider offering a discount on the rent for, say, six weeks if he agrees to stay on for that period. In my experience, you'll get 10 per cent more rent in September than at the end of July so you would soon make up for the discount.

Of course, the holiday rental market has its own peak seasons. In UK seaside and holiday towns the peak will normally be in the summer months or when special local events take place.

In more depressed towns with few employment opportunities and no student or large business population, there will be little seasonality – so one month is probably as busy as any other.

In up-market properties catering to corporate tenants, there will be the same lull in the summer months and the run up to Christmas when businesses effectively shut up and everyone is on holiday.

Another thing to note is that if the weather on the day you advertise is very hot, cold or wet, this will affect the response you get to your advert. Potential tenants don't like trailing round looking at properties if they are going to get sweaty, frozen or soaked.

What to say in your advert

What you say in your advert may depend upon the space available in the publication or website and what that ad space is costing you. Obviously, there are some things that you just *have* to get in and there are some other things that are less essential but, if space and cost allow, are useful to include.

Of course, where the advert is costing you a lot of money, you might be limited to stating just the location and the rent. If you do this, however, you will end up with a lot of enquiries from people for whom the property is unsuitable – e.g. they wanted furnished and your place is unfurnished. You will also get enquiries from people whom *you* may not want – e.g. from people on housing benefit when perhaps you only wanted people in full-time work.

Let's have a look at what you should put in your advert – and why.

STATE THE LOCATION

It's important to state the location accurately and not lie about where it is. Don't say it's central Manchester if it's really in Salford. If you do, it will annoy potential tenants because if there is one thing that tenants *are* clued up about, it's location. If you say it's in central Manchester and it's really in Salford, what will happen is that lots of people just won't turn up. Also, use the new Google Maps Street View facility to show a video of the road it is in.

Some tenants won't turn up for viewings
Don't expect potential tenants to call you and tell you that they are not coming – in my experience only about 30 per cent of tenants will do this.

INCLUDE SOME OTHER DETAILS ABOUT THE PROPERTY
If you are renting a flat and it is self-contained with its own entrance, say so. This feature is particularly attractive to those seeking security and people (like me) who can't abide a smelly hallway full of other people's unwanted junk mail and pizza flyers.

State how many bedrooms it has. If it's a modern property or a warehouse style one, then say so. This is useful as some people prefer older buildings and some prefer modern ones. Also, if it is posh enough, put "apartment" instead of "flat" – it sounds better. Avoid using terms like "duplex" or "conversion" though, especially where potential tenants are non-British as they may not understand these terms.

Tenants nearly always ask how big the rooms are – and you need to have measurements in feet (for Brits and Americans) and metres (for everyone else) ready for when they call. If the rooms are large, say so in the advert.

I would always say "large bedrooms" rather than

"double bedrooms". Suppose you have a two-bed flat and you want to let to a cohabiting couple or two single people. If you put "two double bedrooms" in your ad, you'll attract calls from groups of four single people who want to share the two bedrooms, and this is probably not what you would want, unless, of course, you are happy to have twice the wear and tear!

If it's close to shops, buses or transport say so, and, if space allows, say how far it is in distance rather than minutes. If there is a garden it might be worth saying so. Also, if there is a shower it might be worth stating this. Some people won't even consider a property that doesn't have one. If it has a parking space and it's in an area where parking space is at a premium, then say so, as this is a plus point for many tenants.

STATE WHETHER FURNISHED OR UNFURNISHED

People will ask you about furnishings, so it is useful to put something about this in your ad. The problem is that people have very different ideas about what is meant by the term "furnished".

If you are offering a very up-market property catering to corporate tenants, and particularly for short lets, you may have to go the whole hog and completely furnish the property with TVs, videos and high quality furnishings. For other kinds of property, furnishing to this level isn't expected. Nor is it desirable from your point of view because it will add to your insurance costs, problems managing the inventory, and result in you running around to fix things when they break down. (See also Chapter 5 on Furnishings.)

For "furnished" properties in more run-of-the-mill lets, the following would be expected as a minimum:

washing machine, fridge-freezer, cooker, beds, wardrobes and chest of drawers, sofa, pots and pans, cutlery and cups.

It is worth stating that, just as with the term "furnished", people tend to vary in their understanding of the term "unfurnished". Some think that they will have to provide their own fridge-freezer and washing machine whilst others think that "unfurnished" means that a cooker, a fridge-freezer and a washing machine are provided as standard.

For this reason, where you intend to provide the basic "white goods," use the term "part furnished" or "kitchen equipment furnishings" in your advert to reduce misunderstanding.

STATE WHAT SORT OF TENANTS YOU WANT OR DON'T WANT

Before you advertise, you must decide what sort of tenants you want. The decision about this will depend entirely upon the type of property and your own preferences.

If you have strong views that you don't want tenants who are dependent on housing benefit to pay their rent, then it's probably worth saying so in your advert. Many landlords just put "No Housing Benefit".

You should be aware that even where you put "No Housing Benefit" and "No students" you will still end up with enquiries from people who are in low paid work. I never cease to be amazed by the number of people in part-time cleaning jobs who are seeking to rent a £10,000 per annum property. How would they afford the rent? Would they work twenty hours a day and live off rice? Probably they are planning to sublet to ten of their friends or they will be hoping that housing benefit will pay.

An alternative that works well is to put in your advert, "Full-Time Employed Persons Only" and/or "Deposit and References required". You'd be amazed by the number of people who don't think that they would need to provide any form of referencing or deposit. Stating in your ad that deposit and references are required will cut calls from what I call "No-Credit Time-Wasters".

In addition, to avoid enquiries from people who may want to turn your home into a doss house, you might want to state the number of persons expected to occupy it by stating in your ad, "Suit Couple" or "Three Sharers".

STATE THE RENT

If the custom in the media you are advertising in is to express this in £s per week, then do the same. If the custom is to express it in £s per month then do likewise. However, if you state the rent in £s per week, be aware that you will come across some potential tenants who think that the equivalent monthly rent is exactly four times the weekly rent. If so, politely explain that there are 4.33 weeks (52 weeks divided by 12 months) or 30.42 days (365 days divided by 12 months) in an average month!

INCLUDE YOUR CONTACT TELEPHONE NUMBER

Ideally leave a mobile phone number rather than a landline one. For some reason people are much more likely to leave a message on a mobile phone number than a landline. Why? Perhaps because they know that a message left on a mobile may be responded to more quickly than one left on a landline. You could also leave an email address if space allows.

GIVE AGENTS THE BRUSH OFF

If you want to do it yourself, state "No Agents" in your advert. This will stop the usually less reputable (and desperate) letting agent from calling you to claim that he has twenty "merchant bankers" with glowing references just waiting to rent your property. Just as you should never buy tarmac from the guy who knocks at your door and has some "left over from the council job" so you should never entertain these agents.

However, if you want to have some entertainment, tell him, "Fine. Send your prospective tenants round tonight." And tell him that your fee for taking these surplus tenants off his hands is 20 per cent of the rent. The 20 per cent must be paid upfront of course! That should put him off.

Example of a good advert

Headingley, bright attractive 2-bed apartment, wooden floors, furnished, suit couple or 2/3 sharers, allocated parking. Large rooms, all mod cons. Dep. and refs required. No Housing Benefit or agents. £600pcm. Tel 0777 777 7777.
Email Joe@InsertEmailAddresshere.com

How to screen potential tenants and take references

Once you have got your advert right you should have lots of enquiries coming in. Your next job is therefore to sort the wheat from the chaff or, in other words, to "screen" the respondents.

Just as in selecting candidates for a job, there are three simple stages. Firstly, you do an initial screening when you take phone or email enquiries. Secondly, you screen when you actually meet them. Thirdly, you screen them when you take up their references. Each stage is simple.

Telephone/Email screening

In general, I tend to have my mobile phone switched off and set to taking messages on voice mail. I then review the messages that callers have left and decide who I am going to call back.

This works well for me because I get a lot of calls. This allows me to deal with the calls at a time convenient for me and when I have all the details about the property in front of me.

Of course, if you are in a quieter area, letting larger properties or those that are more exclusive, you will have fewer calls. In these circumstances it's best to take all calls as they are made.

Have a crib sheet with the details about the property on it – room sizes, car parking, distance to transport, level of council tax. You could have this information on computer disk and offer to send it by email. If you are more flash, you could even have your own website with more pictures of the interior of the property.

When people call, have some paper at the ready to note their details – whether employed, where living now, etc.

Take care with your own security. Take a note of their phone numbers including landline phone number, address including postcode, and time of appointment. Check out their landline number by using 1471 and calling them back on it, and leave a note of their details with another person. Check that their address matches their postcode through the Royal Mail website (see Appendix 2). Don't be too paranoid though. If it doesn't match up, there could be an innocent explanation. Ask them.

Finally, have an agreed secret coded message with a friend which you can use to let them know you are in trouble. A good one would be, "I just want to check on the council tax of the property at [state address]."

If you can, arrange appointments at the best time for the property – when it is quiet or when it is brightest!

Tenants love showers (and landlords hate them!)
Most of my flats don't have showers for the good reason that showers often leak, and I can't be bothered with all the hugely time-consuming business of repairing them, filing insurance claims, dealing with tenants who want you to waive their rent while the thing is being fixed and angry neighbours whose ceiling has been ruined. However, I would not tell a potential tenant that my flat does not have a shower unless he was American or Scandinavian (who all seem to insist on them!)

If there is anything that you know about the property that may make it hard to let, you might want to tell your potential tenants when they call. Whether or not you do this will depend on how many other callers you have still to get back to and how desperate you are. However, you also need to be careful as you don't want to put people off!

If the property is more than half a mile from public transport, I would always say this upfront as some tenants are not at all keen on walking further. If you don't tell them how far it is from public transport, you risk them going away, looking it up on a map and just not turning up for the appointment. (I should add that if a property is more than a mile from transport, then you should not have bought it in the first place!)

You may get calls from people on very low incomes

who will obviously have trouble paying the rent unless they get five mates in to share with. So, if you don't want tenants like this, casually ask them where they work and what they do.

If you have someone who is probably not really suitable, then tell him, gently.

Make brief notes on the tenants as you speak to them on the phone and take these with you to the appointment.

I try to avoid doing a viewing with just one tenant, as the sad fact is that, even if you make an appointment in the morning for that evening, about 30 per cent of people won't turn up (or will let you know so late, that you have already journeyed to the property).

If I have only one or two potential tenants coming to a viewing, I would call them just ahead of the viewing to confirm that they are still coming. I *always* reconfirm if the appointment was made the previous day because, for some reason, these ones have a much higher chance of not turning up. Perhaps people don't own diaries! Perhaps they think that it is less rude just not to turn up than to call you and tell you that they have found another property after all.

Some people call when they are minutes away and still fail to turn up. Perhaps they met a friend and went down the pub, perhaps they were hit by a bus, or maybe they were abducted by aliens! Who knows!

I mentioned that it is often a good thing if your property is easy to find. It also helps if the street has a simple, familiar name and if it is listed in the local street atlas.

If you are letting a property that is in a street that has been built at any time in the last twenty years, check if people who are coming to view it have an up-to-date street atlas or map downloaded from the Internet. You'll be amazed by the numbers of people who look for property with a street map or atlas that is years out of date.

Is your property on the local street map?

I once had a property that people always had trouble finding. After a while I realised that although the street was shown on the street map it was not actually listed in the index at the back! Even worse, it was off a road that was also not listed in the index! As a result I had to ensure that I gave each viewer quite detailed directions on how to get there. A bit of a pain!

Even if the road is easy to find you'll get people who will telephone you six times while en route and ask for directions because they haven't got a street map or couldn't be bothered to download one. I would reject these people out of hand as potential tenants – if they haven't got the intelligence to bring along a map with which to find the property, what will they be like as tenants? Chances are that they will call you every time a fuse for a plug needs changing. Save yourself the trouble and avoid them.

Also, avoid people who turn up more than twenty minutes late for a viewing, especially if they don't even bother to think of a good excuse or let you know of the delay in advance.

Interviewing potential tenants

When arranging viewings, get to the property at least fifteen minutes early to turn on lights and heating and generally make the place look as nice as possible.

Stagger viewings about twenty minutes apart. This gives you enough time to meet the individuals and make some notes about them – what they do for a living, where they are living now, how long they have been there, what they are like generally and whether you like them and think you can trust them.

It is best to do this in a discreet informal way and make your notes when they have gone. Your aim should be to seek the following information (ideally for each tenant):

- Name.
- Occupation.
- Where living now.
- Whether living with parents/renting/friends.
- If renting – is this with a letting agency or private landlord?
- For how long have they been living at their current residence?
- Do they have a good relationship with their current landlord?
- What is their contact telephone number or email address?

When meeting tenants it is important to have all the information available that they are likely to need to know about the property. This is where you can make a significant impact compared with most "jobbing landlords" and some letting agencies who can be woefully unprepared to answer tenants' basic questions. Also, if you make no charges to tenants for inventory checks or referencing enquiries, it is worth pointing this out to the tenant. (Some letting agencies still charge sums of up to £250 for "registering" tenants, doing reference enquiries and inventory checks.)

You should know the following:

1. If your advert states the rent as a weekly amount, what this translates to in £s per month.
2. How much the deposit is – this should be a minimum of five weeks' rent, but less than two months' rent.
3. The form of the contract – e.g. "Six-Month Fixed-Term Assured Shorthold Tenancy Renewable at Landlord's Discretion at the End of the Six-Month Term".
4. The current rate of council tax (available from the local council).
5. The estimated cost of electricity, gas and water and whether the water is metered.
6. Where the nearest public transport is, the frequency of service and journey time to major centres.
7. Where the nearest good shops, pubs, restaurants, schools and gyms are.
8. What parking facilities are available and whether any local parking restrictions apply.
9. Any restriction that your tenant should know about – e.g. no pets.
10. What will be included in the way of furnishings.

The last point is very important. Make clear what items will be included in the inventory – i.e. what furnishings will be in the property when the tenant moves in. This is particularly important if you are showing a property where the existing tenant is still in residence and the tenant's furnishings are still in place. Don't allow the prospective tenant to make any assumptions about the inventory. Don't let the tenant think that you will be providing beds or cutlery if you are not.

I have found the best thing is to give tenants a list covering all these points, including details (phone numbers and locations) on all the local services and culture. They can then take this away and study it at their leisure. This makes you look prepared and professional and ensures that there are no doubts and uncertainties to plague the start of your relationship.

How a listing magazine helped me!

I once had a flat in an area of south London that was up and coming but was still perceived by those not in the know to be a haven of criminals and graffiti. For this place I always gave prospective tenants a copy of an article plucked from one of the issues of *Time Out* (a London leisure guide) which extolled the virtues of this part of London. This worked well and won over many younger people, who were keen to live somewhere that was up and coming but still cheap. It's also worth preparing a guide about the property and the area – anything that will help rent it.

When you go into a room, allow the prospective tenant to go in first. You take up space and you want to maximise the impression of space!

Even if you think you have found a good tenant, I would continue to show other candidates because people sometimes change their minds. It normally takes about two days to complete the take up of references. If, in this time, the tenant you had lined up changes his mind, then you have to start again. And if your property is already vacant then you will be into a void period with no rental income. If you have got someone else lined up, then hopefully he can step into the breach.

Taking up references
The third stage is to take up references. What references you check and how thoroughly you go about this is probably the most important thing you will do as a landlord. If you don't believe this just ask landlords who have suffered with bad tenants – they will all agree that, if they had taken more care in checking their tenants out, they would probably not have had problems.

The purpose of references is to confirm that the person is who he says he is, that he can afford the rent and that he doesn't have a history of not honouring his commitments in the past.

If you don't bother referencing a tenant properly, you will eventually end up losing a lot of money. Just in case you think that referencing is not important because you could kick out a bad tenant the next day, I would urge you to read the box on page 152.

What references you should ask for will depend on the type of tenant you are seeking. However, the following are essential for an employed tenant and should be obtained for each person.

1. An employer's reference.
2. A reference from a previous (and preferably last but one) landlord.
3. Proof of identity.
4. Proof of current address.
5. A satisfactory credit reference report.
6. Proof of permit or visa entitling the tenant to work in the United Kingdom (non-EU nationals only).

A prospective tenant should be able to get all these references within two working days. If he is unable to get them within this time frame, tell him that he risks the property being let to someone else.

There are some exceptions to this list. If you are letting to tenants who are depending on housing benefit to pay their rent, then they may not be in full-time employment and therefore you will not need to ask for an employer's reference. In such circumstances, the other checks are even more important. I shall discuss each of the references in turn.

EMPLOYER REFERENCES

The employer's reference should state how long the person has been employed, the nature of the employment contract – e.g. permanent/temporary, the salary and a statement that the person is not under notice to leave.

To save time you should ask your tenant to get this reference from his employer himself rather than you writing to the employer. When you get the reference back, read it carefully. Does it give you all the information you asked for? Ideally it should be from the Personnel or Human Resources Department but a reference provided by a senior manager is usually just as good.

You should *always* telephone to verify the reference. Rather than telephone the referee's direct line, go through the main switchboard of the company, check the referee's job title and only then ask to be put through to the referee. Then identify yourself and check that he provided the reference and validate what it says. All employers should be happy to do this for you.

In phoning the employer and checking the referee's job title, you are just confirming that the reference is not written by a mate of your prospective tenant.

The cost of a bad tenant

If you have a tenant who doesn't pay the rent, the only way to get him out is to apply to a county court to start possession proceedings and have him evicted. You cannot "send the boys round" or in any way harass the tenant by calling at 4 am or cutting off his water, etc. If you do this, it is a criminal offence and you'll be the one in trouble.

You can only start court action for eviction after a period of two months of unpaid rent. In addition to this, you will have to pay a court fee to start the action. If your paperwork is OK, the court will grant an order telling the tenant to leave. (A Notice to Quit.) If the tenant doesn't leave by the date in the Notice, then you'll have to pay another fee for bailiffs to come in and remove him. If it goes this far, you'll lose about four months' rent as well as court fees too. (If the tenant persuades the court he has a valid excuse not to attend a hearing or a counter-claim, the whole thing can drag on longer.)

During this time you will, of course, have to pay the mortgage and all the usual running costs of the property. Additionally, you'll almost certainly find that the tenant has not been paying any of his other bills too and you'll have to deal with a small mountain of post from his debt collectors. He may also have damaged electricity and gas meters to obtain a free supply. Some tenants even deliberately damage the property or at least leave it in a dirty condition. Bad tenants don't make great neighbours, so you may also have to deal with angry neighbours too.

If you want to recover the money you are owed, this is a separate court action with additional costs, and your chances of recovery are not high unless your tenant is in the UK, is traceable and has a job.

As well as the cost of evicting a bad tenant, there is also the time and stress. So pick your tenant with care. (For more on bad tenants and eviction, see Chapter 9.)

If in doubt, don't let to them
I once had a set of references from a prospective tenant who I wasn't sure about. He couldn't provide an address history.

He had provided wage slips showing a modest income but I was a little concerned that he might struggle to pay the rent and I had a slight doubt about him anyway. When I telephoned to validate the employer's reference, it was my tenant who answered the phone. What was really odd was that he just picked it up and said, "Hello." There was no company name given and it didn't sound professional. That night I went round to visit his company. Although the tenant had described a large international export business, the company was actually on a tiny site under a railway arch. I decided he was just too risky and decided not to let to him.

Many people nowadays work on a contract basis. If so, they should be able to provide you with evidence of their current contracts. Where someone works on a freelance basis for many clients, you should ask for evidence of regular income from his bank statements over a period of at least six months. His agent or accountant may be able to provide proof of past and/or future income too. Clients may be prepared to provide proof of future work in the pipeline. These references should be followed up.

If he has his own company, ask to see its last two years' reports and accounts. If it hasn't been trading for that long, you will need to look for other evidence that he can pay the rent, so the other references listed here will need to be very good.

It is important to check if what the tenant said to you

when you met him ties in with what his employment references say. That's why it's useful to make notes of even those casual "getting to know you" conversations on the phone or when he first came to view your property. If there is a discrepancy, gently probe further. If you have real doubts, walk away!

PREVIOUS LANDLORD REFERENCE

A previous landlord reference, especially one from a *good* respectable letting agent, can be very reassuring and, if I had to choose between two sets of tenants with the same references but one had a previous landlord reference and one didn't, I would let to the one with the previous reference every time.

Ideally this should be from the landlord before his current one as his current one may be prepared to say anything just to get rid of him.

The reference should state the start and end dates of the tenancy, the rent amount, whether this rent was always paid on time, his conduct as a tenant and whether the referee would recommend the tenant as being reliable, honest and trustworthy.

Again, always phone to validate it. If it's from a large letting agency, always call the main switchboard number first and validate the referee. If the agency is local, go and see them. You might find that when you speak to the landlord he is not as glowing about the tenant as he was in writing.

Of course, not all people can provide a previous landlord reference for various good reasons. For example, they may have never rented before or their landlord may be hard to get hold of or uncooperative.

Therefore, one of the things I always try to find out

when I first meet tenants is where they are living now and whether they are currently renting. If they say they are renting, I always ask them what their landlord is like. I have met quite a few sets of tenants who have said that the reason that they are moving out is that their landlord is awful – he doesn't fix things, they have had a hole in their wall for six weeks and damp in their living room for months. They can never get hold of him and have had enough.

The chances are that these people will be unable to get a reference from their landlord. Of course, if they are genuine and their landlord is the idiot that they say he is, then they will probably make good tenants who will appreciate a good landlord like you!

Naturally, you have to be alert to the fact that the reason that they cannot get a previous landlord reference is because it was they who were awful and so their last landlord will not give them a reference. Some tenants might be so awful that a previous landlord will say anything in a reference if it helps to get rid of the problem onto someone else. Unfortunately, there is not much that you can do about this. After all, it's very unlikely that you could ever prove that a landlord gave a misleading reference and, even if you could, then so what? Giving a misleading or untrue reference is hardly something the police will be interested in. That is why a reference from the landlord *before the last one* is usually the best of all.

If the reference is from a landlord in another country who doesn't speak English, you will have to find someone who speaks the same language to validate the reference. Make the effort. It only takes a call and will give you peace of mind.

Finally, you can check whether the previous landlord

really owns the property he says he let to the tenant by running a check on the Land Registry website for about £3. This is a very useful "background check" that few landlords or agents do.

PROOF OF IDENTITY

Proof of identity is a must. Ask for sight of an official original document proving the person's identity – usually this will be the person's passport or new-style driving licence or any other official document that has his photograph on it. Keep a copy of the photo and a record of the passport or identity number.

CHECKING ADDRESSES AND THE CREDIT REFERENCE

The reason for checking the tenant's current and previous addresses is linked to the running of a credit reference check.

I normally ask to see the last three utility bills, mobile phone bills (or even better bank statements) in that person's name to check his most recent address. A bank statement for that person's *current* account can be particularly useful as this will give you an idea of whether he is in credit and whether income from a job is being paid into the account and rent is being paid out. Used in this way it acts as an additional check on the employer's reference.

You can do a basic credit reference check on a tenant for less than £15 and there are a number of suppliers who provide this service. Normally, the credit referencing company will issue a form on which you fill in the full name of the prospective tenant, his date of birth and his addresses over the last three years. Some companies will also ask you to state the amount of the rent.

You simply complete the form and get the tenant to sign it. The credit referencing company can normally send you a report within the hour and you can use it to assess whether the tenant is a good risk. More importantly the report should tell you whether this tenant has something negative in his credit history like a County Court Judgment – i.e. a debt that he hasn't paid.

You need to use common sense to interpret a credit report, but it also helps to know how credit scoring works. I'll try to explain.

A person's credit score is basically a reflection of how he runs his finances. If you own your own home and have lots of accounts on which you honour your commitments then you will have a very good score. You could, of course, have lots of overdrawn accounts but, as long as you are meeting repayments, then your score will still be good. Conversely, a young student, who has been renting for a few years, hasn't bothered to register on the electoral roll, has moved addresses a few times, doesn't pay the utility bills where he is living and has a short credit history, will have a low score.

Therefore be careful when using credit scores. If you are letting property to young recent graduates, the chances are that they will have low credit scores. The key thing to look out for here is that they don't have a negative credit history – i.e. outstanding County Court Judgments. However, if their score is particularly low, you might want to seek a guarantor such as a parent.

If someone has a County Court Judgment against him, he should tell you before you do the credit reference enquiry. In some cases it may be that the debt is due to a past business failure that is about to be cleared. Ultimately, you will have to weigh up what your prospective tenant tells you about previous debts with the other information and the other references and come to a decision. The key thing is, if in doubt, don't let to him.

If you are letting to foreign nationals who have recently moved to the UK, credit referencing is of more limited use because most credit referencing companies still don't have lots of data from foreign countries. (If you are deciding which referencing service to use, it is worth asking them which countries they cover.) This is particularly relevant in the big cities and at the lower end of the market where the majority of potential tenants may be from overseas.

NON-EU NATIONALS – WORK PERMITS

If you are letting to someone who is a national of a country outside the European Union, you should check his entitlement to work in the UK because, if he can't work, he probably won't be able to pay you rent!

OTHER CHECKS

Some landlords ask for bank status enquiries in which they write to the tenant's bank and ask for a report on their creditworthiness. I wouldn't bother for the reason that the banks take far too long to respond and the wording of their responses is usually confusing and vague. Of course, another alternative is to ask your prospective tenant for sight of his bank statement. Most tenants are happy to comply.

Some referencing companies offer a service where they do a credit reference enquiry and also check the employer's and previous landlord's reference – basically doing the whole thing for you. However, I can't see the point of paying a third party to check employer's and landlord's references when that is something that you can do much quicker yourself and at the cost of a couple of phone calls.

If you are letting to students, their parents should sign the tenancy agreement as guarantors. This means that the parents will be jointly and severally responsible to pay the whole rent if the student doesn't. All the usual checks should be done on the parent as you would do for any other potential tenant – however, there is probably no need to check parents' bank statements if you can establish that they own a home in the UK. You can check if they own their home through the Land Registry (see Appendix 2). Guarantors should be used for any person who, for whatever reason, can't provide all the references you need. This would include the self-employed whose real income may be greater than can be proven in a bank statement. Guarantors must be UK home-owners.

Finally, it's also useful to have a record of the tenant's National Insurance number.

GUT FEEL

When making a decision about whether to let to someone, use each of the references and exercise common sense. However, the most important thing is probably gut feel as you'll rarely find the tenant whose references are immaculate in every way.

If the references are in any way deficient or you have only slight doubts, you could ask for three to six months' rent in advance. This could be in addition to the provision of a guarantor.

Don't lose sight of the fact that the vast majority of prospective tenants are basically honest and only about 2 per cent will be cheats and con artists. However, be particularly wary of well-dressed and plausible-looking people who just *have to* move in today. They'll always promise that they will have the money tomorrow. If you let these people into your property, you'll get no rent and you will have a very difficult job of getting your property back, as they know every trick in the book and will use the system to their advantage. You have been warned!

If you have a nagging doubt about someone, you *must* walk away even if your property is proving hard to let and *never* let someone in to your property until you have obtained cleared funds for both the deposit and rent.

The good news is that if you use a referencing system such as the one I've described, you will almost certainly avoid the bad tenants. Bad tenants know that they can't provide the documentation required by a proper reference check and, when faced with one, will go away and seek a more gullible landlord elsewhere.

LETTING TO COMPANIES

What about letting to companies? First check whether it is a limited company and assess its financial worth by obtaining a copy of its report and accounts from Companies House. If there is any doubt about the company's stability then put the tenancy in the tenant's name rather than the company's, especially if he has assets like a house elsewhere. Then, check the individual's references as you would any other person. Insist on a home-owning guarantor if you are worried.

Many of the more up-market fully furnished properties are let on short-term contracts to companies direct. Avoid letting to a foreign-based company as it would be expensive to pursue a claim abroad – again it would be better to let to the individual rather than the company; and be wary of letting to workers for foreign governments who may have diplomatic immunity.

Don't accept a "letter of guarantee" from a company; insist on a deposit and cleared funds before anyone moves in. See also the section in Chapter 6 on company lets.

LETTING TO INDIVIDUALS IN A HOUSE SHARE

You may be letting to individuals in a shared house. This entails more work than where you let out a whole property, as people will be coming and going more frequently. Each person may have his own agreement to let a room.

All the tenants should be checked and referenced in the same way as before and, to save your time, you should put the responsibility on them to find replacement tenants when they move out (still subject to all your reference checks and agreement of course). Also, be aware that the property could be counted as an HMO – with possibly more regulations to comply with. For more on this see Chapter 5.

WHAT IF THEY ARE ON HOUSING BENEFIT/LOCAL HOUSING ALLOWANCE?

If a tenant is on housing benefit (HB), some or all of the rent will be paid to the tenant by the State. HB tenants can be profitable and problem-free but care is needed. The main problem is the delays in processing applications so the tenant should apply to the housing benefit officer well before the planned move-in date. Tenants should sign a letter of authority allowing the HB staff to talk to the landlord regarding the progress of the application. Keep in mind that the amount paid by the authority will be limited by the size of the property required for the tenant's needs – i.e. a single person aged over 35 with no kids will only get HB payment for a one-bed not a three-bed flat! Also, different areas have different rates.

It's worth keeping on good terms with the HB Office at all times. (Please also see Chapter 8, page 168, for more on managing HB tenants and Chapter 9, page 214, for how to deal with problems with HB tenants.)

Final steps and what happens on move-in day

Assuming you are happy with the potential tenants you should ask them to pay a cash reservation fee of three weeks' rent as proof of their commitment to proceed. You should emphasise on your receipt that this is non-refundable if they change their minds for any reason and decide not to move in or fail to show up on the agreed move-in date.

At this stage you should give them a *draft* copy of the tenancy agreement and ask them to read it through carefully. I have emphasised the words draft, because you should not sign the formal tenancy agreement until they have moved in and have paid you the balance of the deposit (full deposit less holding deposit already paid) and the first month's rent. Endorse that it's a draft or specimen tenancy agreement by writing *draft* or *specimen* across each page of the agreement.

You can then make the final arrangements prior to the tenants' moving in. This will involve them contacting the electricity, gas, water, phone and council tax people. I also ask tenants to ensure that their own contents insurance has accidental damage cover included – so that their insurance company can pick up the bill if they spill red wine on my carpet.

I always ask tenants to ensure that they have set up their standing order and to make sure the rent payments are in my account on time. With some banks it can still take three working days for money to go from one person's account to another. Therefore, to allow for this and the additional effect of weekends and bank holidays, I ask tenants to ensure that the money leaves their account six calendar days before it is due in mine.

On move-in date, tell tenants in advance that the formalities will take about an hour. Agree and sign a detailed inventory check, preferably one done by an independent inventory clerk – which should include date stamped photos and even videos these days – and note any marks, chips or damages to every item in the inventory or any carpets or walls and describing every item of furnishing in detail. Ideally, take photos and a video to prove not just the condition of the property but also the meter readings in case of disputes later. Show them how everything works using the House Guide as explained in Chapter 6.

Oh no! I can't find a tenant! What do I do?
What you must avoid is the dreaded void period, where you don't have a tenant but of course you still have to pay the mortgage and all the other bills. Firstly, do not panic. Secondly, examine the possible causes of why you aren't managing to let your property.

If you are advertising it yourself and getting few calls, ask yourself the following questions:

Is it advertised in the right publication(s)? Look at other places advertised in the same publication. If these properties are much smarter than yours or vice versa, perhaps you are in the wrong publication. Would a better photo help? Remember too, your rent should be less than similar advertised properties. Other properties that have been advertised for weeks on end are, by definition, at too high a rent.

Are there too many properties of the same type on the market? If so, can you differentiate yours in some way? If not, then you are going to have to cut the rent.

Is it the time of year? Over the summer and at Christmas it goes very quiet in most big towns, especially college towns. Hang on till mid August or January.

Is the weather too hot, cold or wet? When the weather is very horrible (or very nice), tenants don't go looking for accommodation.

Are you excluding groups of people unnecessarily? For example, if your ads exclude students, you might like to consider them. If you are worried about students causing more damage to your property you could always ask for a higher deposit, do reference checks on students' parents, make them guarantors for the rent or restrict the let to more mature (and hopefully more responsible) post grad students.

If you are getting enquiries and/or viewings but no conversion, perhaps your advert is "over selling". Maybe there is something else wrong with the property. Perhaps it needs to be decorated better? Contact people who have rejected it and ask them for their honest opinions.

If you are using a letting agent and not getting the property let, get a friend to pose as a potential tenant and see how your agent performs. If he performs poorly, get a new agent.

Finally, they should pay the balance of the deposit and the first month's rent in cash. I would advise against accepting a banker's or building society draft as there is always a small risk it could be stolen or fraudulent. You should both sign the tenancy agreement of which there should be two original copies – one for the landlord and one for the tenant. It's worth also taking next of kin details in case anything should happen to the tenant.

8

HOW TO MANAGE
THE TENANCY

How to manage the tenants

After a couple of months, go and visit your tenants and take a look at the property. You can use this opportunity to run through the House Guide again (see Chapter 6) to see that they know what to do in an emergency. After that, if everything is OK, I tend to leave my tenants alone apart from annual check-ups. My view is if they're paying the rent, they're probably also looking after the property too and will know to let me know if anything is wrong. The only exception is if a letting agent is managing it, where I'd insist on visits and reports being done each quarter.

Only go to the property after arranging an appointment, except if there is an emergency that needs fixing immediately and you can't wait for the tenant to be on site.

Check your bank account on the date the tenants' money is due. If it isn't there contact them straightaway. It may be just an error at their bank. If this is the excuse, to avoid further delays get the tenants to pay cash, either direct to you or in cash at a branch of your own bank. This will ensure you'll have the money by the next business day. If they are late paying, don't accept a cheque or a re-sent standing order as it takes too long to clear. If a tenant says it's his bank's fault, then his bank should re-send it on "same day clearance" and pick up the cost too.

If a tenant still hasn't paid after a week, then telephone or visit. Be firm and polite. If the tenant makes a formal complaint to anyone about you, stop calling round and make future rent demands in writing. I'll explain more about what to do with problem tenants in Chapter 9.

More up-market properties, especially those that are fully furnished, let on short-term contacts or to companies, will command higher rents, but will require more management because tenants' expectations will be that much higher and the more frequent changeover of tenants will mean more checking in and out. Your challenge will be to meet tenants' higher expectations whilst keeping voids to a minimum.

How to manage housing benefit/ local housing allowance (LHA) tenants

Tenants on housing benefit need to be managed slightly differently. Most lettings to housing benefit tenants work well once they've been set up and the tenants tend to stay longer too, thus reducing void periods and re-letting costs. But getting the forms filled in right and understanding how the process works can be hard work for the novice.

In some areas housing benefit officers take ages to process new claims. In other areas they are much more efficient. A few years ago, one city council in the north west of England was taking an incredible 183 days to process them! If this happens, formally ask for an interim payment. The council will then either have to pay in full or make an interim payment fourteen days after having all the information necessary.

The Government has recently completed the process of replacing housing benefit with the new local housing allowance (LHA). The key difference under the new LHA system is that tenants (not the landlord) will get money paid direct to them. Of course, this change clearly increased the risk that the tenant spends the money on something other than rent and, unsurprisingly, landlords don't think it was a great idea. However, if the tenant is in eight weeks' rent arrears or they are deemed to be vulnerable, the landlord can still be paid direct. As processing can be slow, don't wait for eight weeks' arrears to build before applying for direct payment – notify the housing benefit officer there is a problem as early as you can!

Where the council is paying the benefit direct to you and the tenant is later found to be ineligible, the council may try to recover the money from you. In order to safeguard your position, visit the property regularly during the tenancy to ensure that the tenant hasn't vacated and that there aren't any other circumstances that could affect their benefit. Examples may be someone else moving into the property or the tenant getting a different job. Again, any such visits must be arranged with the tenants in advance. Provided that you have done all you can to check that no fraud is going on, it will be hard for the housing benefit office to claim back overpayments from you. Most overpayment claims can be resisted successfully. See Chapter 9, page 214, for more on how to do this.

How much local housing allowance a tenant gets will depend on rents in the local area (each area of the country is divided into Broad Market Rental Areas) and the size of the property he is deemed to need. Use the look-up tables at the LHA Direct website to find out the maximum levels paid in your area.

Bear in mind that the now massive bill for housing benefit is a political football and the new coalition government has pledged to cut the cost by reducing LHA payments. All the same, if you get these lets right and can deal with potentially more difficult tenants, it can be very lucrative and worth the effort. To get the full facts on Local Housing Allowance download and read the government document "Housing Benefit Local Allowance Guidance Manual".

How to manage a letting agent

In Chapter 7, I explained what sort of things to look for in a letting agent who will just *find* a tenant for you. Of course, such agents can also be used to *manage* your property too, which may be useful if you live a long way away and don't know any local plumbers. If you're going to use an agency for management, you must be clear about what level of service it is going to provide. You can get an idea by asking the agency the following questions:

1. How quickly after they receive the tenant's money will it be in your account?
2. How frequently will they pay visits to inspect the property?
3. What will they look for when they do inspection visits?
4. If maintenance work is required, whom will they

call? Do they have their own maintenance people or will they just get someone out of the phone book?

5. Are their maintenance people members of the appropriate professional bodies, e.g. NICEIC for electricians, IPHE, etc, for plumbers, Gas Safe Registered for gas? Do they check their membership?

6. Will they arrange the annual gas safety check?

7. Do they have a special telephone number for tenants to call for maintenance out of normal office hours?

8. How quickly will someone be on site if there is an emergency such as a burst pipe?

9. Do they request an estimate for routine works first?

10. Will they clear the cost of work with you or just go ahead? Above what amount will they request your authorization?

11. Can they advise what the average cost of a sample of typical maintenance jobs is? (Are the costs reasonable?)

12. What money float do they require you to provide to cover maintenance?

13. How will you be invoiced for maintenance work?

14. How frequently will they send statements?

15. Are they members of the RICS, NAEA, NALS, ARLA or UKALA schemes for agents? (These umbrella organisations may operate a bonding scheme protecting your money in the event the agent goes bust.)

16. What are their procedures at the end of the tenancy, including the hand-over of the deposit?

17. How will they prove they have protected tenants' deposits in one of the schemes? You are responsible for this so make sure they have done it!

They probably won't have the answers to each question or, if they do, they won't have documented procedures for their staff to follow in each case. However, from their responses, you'll be able to assess their degree of professionalism and whether your property is safe in their hands. If they haven't got a clue, go to another agent.

A letting agency should earn its management fee by doing regular inspections and should be prepared to talk through your House Guide with your tenants, demonstrating how things work and what to do in the event of an emergency. They should be able to show you a list of things they look for on inspection visits. Ideally, this should be a pre-prepared list that can be given to anyone doing inspections. It should include a list of things to look for which might indicate damp, overflowing pipes, etc. A really good agent would complete a report after each inspection visit and send it to you.

Be wary of getting an agent involved with arranging emergency repairs. Most agents say they have a network of competent tradesmen who can deal with emergencies and other work at reasonable cost. However, many experienced landlords think all some of them do is get out the *Yellow Pages* to find someone, then stick a percentage on top and charge you for it. So, where the work isn't covered by insurance, and some of it won't be, you could just end up paying more than if you arranged the work yourself. Also, since many letting agents don't provide a twenty-four-hour emergency service, if the problem occurs at night or on a Sunday, the tenant will end up calling you anyway!

The reality is that there isn't much money in managing lettings. Where a big agent has a smart office for lettings, it is probably being paid for from the more lucrative property sales side of the business! Since margins are tight and the work dull and admin heavy, many letting agents will be tempted to cut corners by sending the office dimwit to do an inspection or "forget" to do it at all.

If you ask all the questions above and get sensible answers, you'll have a good agent who will treat your account with respect but you'll still need to keep on top of them. Letting agency staff move often, so don't leave new staff in any doubt about the standard of service you expect!

How to manage maintenance

Too many landlords fail to manage their properties properly and when faced with emergencies they often do the wrong thing and end up paying out far more than they need to.

As a landlord you have a duty to keep your property in good repair, so this means spending some time managing people who come to fix things when they go wrong. If you live close to your property, are good with your hands and have the time, you can of course do it yourself. However, there are some exceptions. If you aren't a Gas Safe registered gas engineer you can't try to fix gas appliances. If you do, you are breaking the law. Also, most significant electrical work now requires a qualified electrician.

For other things too, it's important to know what you're doing, so, if you don't, get the job done by a professional who does! They'll also get it done in half the time. If you find a good tradesman, pay his bill on time and cultivate a good relationship. Then, when the big freeze comes you should be near the front of the queue. If you've got a number of properties, try getting your tradesmen to agree a service level agreement and a fixed price list for emergency and other call outs.

Get things fixed as soon as possible. If there is going to be an unavoidable delay, tell your tenants as soon as possible. Also, let them know in advance when you or your tradesmen will be on site and never go in without making a prior arrangement unless it's an emergency. If you don't fix things quickly you'll lose tenants. If you don't fix them at all, you could get a court order compelling you to carry out repairs and you'll have to pay court costs too.

If the property (or part of it) is uninhabitable, for example following a leak, give your tenants a rent reduction or waiver. You generate good will and the lost rent or cost of alternative accommodation should be covered by insurance anyway!

Dealing with leaks and heating problems
Water damage in a property can be very expensive. The most common problems are to do with showers, boilers, pumps, dripping taps, leaking pipes and toilet overflows. Things like dripping taps should take no more than forty-five minutes to fix. Your tenants are, of course, your front line for dealing with emergencies like a burst main or boiler leak and they should know what to do to minimise damage. See Chapter 6, for what should be in a tenant's emergency "House Guide".

Let's assume your tenants have followed the instructions in their House Guide and have stopped the flow of running water. The next step is to get the thing permanently fixed. There are a number of options here.

The initial response of many landlords is to get an emergency plumber from the phone directory or, if there is a management contract with a letting agent, call him. Calling someone from the *Yellow Pages* may be expensive and there is no guarantee of competency. However, if you *must* do this, don't use people who charge "by the hour". Insist on getting them to agree a fixed quote (not an estimate!) for the repair. (You will, of course, have to pay the first call out fee which should also be agreed in advance.)

Usually, the best bet is to call your insurance company as resulting damage is normally claimable anyway! These days many insurers have emergency trades people who'll do an initial fix, and often some of the cost of this work is covered by the buildings insurance. If it's not covered then use your own tradesmen.

It's possible to take out a separate "Home Emergencies" contract to cover household emergencies. Schemes on offer from some utility companies cover a number of contingencies from plumbing and gas central heating to electrical appliances. However, these usually don't cover replacement of appliances, kitchen and bathroom fixtures, tap washers, showers, the mains electricity supply or rewiring. If your insurance policy offers emergency cover free of charge then it's not worth bothering with a separate Home Emergencies contract.

Landlords with two or more properties should have a reliable plumber and qualified gas engineer on their books. Unfortunately, getting a good one who is also available is as rare as finding rocking horse manure. To get a good one, ask for recommendations from other people or ask the trade bodies. For water and heating, there is the Institute of Plumbing and Heating Engineering (IPHE) and the Association of Plumbing and Heating Contractors (APHC). See Appendix 2.

In the case of the IPHE you can complain to them if the contractor's work is shoddy or their fee too high. The IPHE has a professional standards committee (including a member from Trading Standards) that can look into unresolved complaints, and members who fail to correct shoddy work can be struck off. Don't forget that being on the Gas Safe Register is a requirement for anyone working with gas but it gives no guarantees at all when it comes to plumbing.

If you have a flat, you'll probably have to contact the freeholder's managing agent, even if it's just to register the insurance claim or get into another property to stop a leak. Many landlords say that their managing agents are good at just one thing – collecting the ground rent/service charges and are pretty useless when things go wrong. If this sounds like your freeholder's agent, think about buying your freehold, applying for commonhold or getting the freeholder to get a new managing agent, preferably one who is a member of the Association of Residential Managing Agents. (See Appendix 2.)

Most leases require the freeholder's consent to major works, so if you have suffered from a leak from an upstairs flat that was caused by works, check that the freeholder's consent was given. If not, the freeholder should take action against the upstairs flat owner.

Problems with water leaks in flats are worse where a flat has just bare floorboards because water will pass straight through, causing more damage. If your tenants are continually flooded by careless occupiers of flats above them, check if the flooring in the offending flat complies with the lease as many leases have a requirement that flats be kept carpeted. Also, keep a diary record of all flood damage, with photos as supporting evidence. If problems continue, try to get the managing agent to instruct a solicitor to enforce the lease provisions.

Often leases have penalties for persistent careless behaviour, and freeholders can ultimately forfeit the flat owner's lease. However, getting a managing agent/freeholder actually to do anything is often a challenge in itself! Finally, don't forget, within the terms of most leases, that managing agents/freeholders and residents in neighbouring flats have the right to enter another flat to do emergency repairs, if the problem is affecting them.

Get some heaters
It's worth investing in some electric heaters which can be made available for tenants, if their heating breaks down in the middle of winter and there is a delay of a day or so in getting it fixed.

Getting a new boiler
As central heating boilers get old the cost of maintaining and repairing increases and most boilers have a life of no more than fifteen years. Normally, it's best to replace with the same energy source as before. In rural areas, there may be no mains gas anyway so oil or electricity will be the only sources of heating. Where the property is small, a "combi" boiler which in summer heats the water only when taps are on will be best. Combis also don't require a hot water tank, thus saving on space but an under powered one can take longer to run a bath as the water is heated through the burners.

Look for a boiler carrying the Energy Efficiency

Recommended logo which guarantees that the boiler has met strict efficiency criteria. See Appendix 2 for useful website addresses.

The new condensing boilers are cheaper to run because they extract the remaining heat from the water cycle when it returns to the boiler for reuse. They are roughly about 90 to 95 per cent efficient at converting fuel into heat whereas a ten- to fifteen-year-old boiler may be only 65 per cent efficient. It's worth checking out the tax breaks available to landlords under the Government's Landlords' Energy Savings Allowance and what's available from the Government in your area at the Energy Saving Trust's website at www.est.org.uk.

Non combi boilers are best where the boiler is likely to be used a lot, for example in properties with more than one bathroom. If space is limited, a condensing combi might be the best option. If you have a new efficient boiler, tell any prospective tenants as it will be they who'll enjoy savings on their fuel bills. If they are deciding between renting your property and another, this could just tilt the balance in your favour!

When installing a new boiler, put in a timer and thermostats to make them even more efficient. If it's a gas boiler, consider having carbon monoxide sensors fitted too, this is a good and cheap safety feature.

Finally, landlords entering into new tenancy agreements from October 2008 will have by law to provide their tenants with an Energy Performance Certificate (EPC) showing the energy efficiency of the property. The certificates are valid for ten years and they cost from around £50 to do. Search for "Domestic Energy Assessors" on the Internet to find an assessor.

Dealing with drainage problems

The drains in your property including the pipe connecting to the sewer are your responsibility and your plumber should be able to look after your drainage, whereas the water company is responsible for mains drainage. If the problem is somewhere between property and road, but it's unclear exactly where, I've found the water company will usually do the job. For flats, the pipes serving your flat are your responsibility and not that of the block. However, where the pipe serves more than one flat, the maintenance responsibility belongs to the freeholder and their managing agent.

Things to check as part of your maintenance programme
- Check that the water stop valve can be opened and closed easily. If it sticks, spray on some WD40.
- Clear drains, down pipes and gutters of leaves and moss.
- Lift manhole covers to check if drains are flowing freely.
- Lag any boiler pipes that are exposed.

Dealing with damp problems

People often worry about damp and mould unnecessarily as often the cause is just condensation resulting from poor ventilation and is common in house to flat conversions. A simple solution is to install an extractor fan in the bathroom and get tenants to air the property regularly. If necessary, put in some air bricks. Other causes are plumbing leaks, localised failure of the damp proof course and water penetration from blocked gutters. Sort out the possible causes first and if there is still a problem get a quote from a few independent damp surveyors.

Dealing with electrical problems
Get a properly qualified electrician to check thoroughly any property you buy and to deal with any problems that come up. As part of your regular maintenance cycle, check smoke detector batteries and lightly vacuum the detector elements once a year. Better still, put in hard-wired smoke detectors (i.e. fitted into the mains) on each floor, including one near to the kitchen. This overcomes the problem of tenants neglecting to replace old batteries. Ensure doors are fire-resistant. Appliance cover is available for things like washing machines, though many are poor value for money as nowadays equipment rarely fails in the first five years.

Dealing with pest problems
Ensure tenants are not leaving food out first then if the problem persists call the local council. They'll often deal with the problem free of charge or for a small fee.

How to manage a problem neighbour

Just because it's a rented property, don't think that the fact that the neighbours are awful won't matter to you. It will matter to your tenants, so it will end up mattering to you if they are made so unhappy they end up moving out.

Nobody should have to put up with neighbours from hell and the Government now seems to be taking the problem seriously by issuing criminal behaviour orders. However, they are only applied when things are really very bad. In most cases, you'll have to try to work out the problem yourself.

The first thing is try to talk reasonably to the neighbour to see if he can stop doing whatever is causing the problem. Only if the problem persists should you take the matter further. If it's noise, contact the Environmental Health section at your local council. If the offending property is rented and the occupier is breaching the lease, tell his landlord. An up-to-date address for the owner might be listed in the Land Registry (see Appendix 2). If it's a flat in the same building as yours and with the same freeholder, try to get the managing agent to take action. Keep a diary log of all events and correspondence, including phone calls.

Complaints about neighbours must be declared when you come to sell the property, even if that complaint has been resolved. You're also supposed to declare any complaint made about you and any you've made about the freeholder or their agents. If the complaint has been resolved, this will probably satisfy most potential purchasers. If the complaint is ongoing, it may make it harder to sell and could affect the price you get too.

Lots of people don't declare complaints or disputes in the hope their buyer won't find out. This is risky because it may come to light when the buyer moves in and meets the neighbours. In the worst case you could even end up being sued. So, if you're thinking of selling the property soon anyway, consider whether it's really worth making a formal complaint at all.

If it's your tenant who is causing a nuisance, talk to the neighbours and deal with their concerns as soon as possible. I once made the mistake of not doing this and it ended up costing me money. It was on my very first letting and I had a tenant from hell. (I'm glad to say it was the last time I had a tenant like this and my experience with him later inspired this book!)

When it's not worth complaining
I used to own a top floor flat in a converted house where the front garden was a mess. It put off potential tenants and would do the same for any potential buyer of my flat. The garden belonged to the basement flat whose owner didn't seem to be interested.

I considered sending a formal letter to the managing agent asking him to write to the owner to get her to tidy it up. However, I knew I'd have to declare this when I came to sell the property. So, instead, I decided that whenever I wanted to re-let my flat, I'd just go around and tidy the garden myself. It took about two hours each time. One day, the owner of the basement flat popped out and gave me money to cover my time and trouble. I hadn't expected it, and, although it wasn't much, it made me feel better about the hassle!

My problem tenant left eventually. Later, when I re-let it, there was a small leak in my flat. Unfortunately, it wasn't detected quickly and it caused some damage to the flat below me which prompted the neighbour who lived there and his brother to turn up at my own home one day, demanding all sorts of compensation. They looked pretty hard cases and it wasn't a pleasant experience. I had to pay all their vastly inflated damage claims which luckily were mostly picked up by my insurance company. I reflected that if I had offered the neighbour more tea and sympathy when the problem tenant had been around, he may have been more accommodating when the leak happened.

How to end your tenancy

How to give them notice

An assured shorthold tenancy will end at the end of the fixed term (unless both parties accept an extension). However, even where a fixed term of, say, six months exists, you *still* need to give the tenant at least two months' notice. Let me explain. Suppose on 1 January you set up a fixed six-month tenancy – i.e. ending on 30 June. You can't just walk into the property on 30 June. You would *still* need by 30 April to issue notice to leave. I know it sounds stupid, but that's the law!

In order to avoid forgetting to issue the notice to leave, landlords who definitely want to end a tenancy at the end of a fixed term, automatically just issue a notice to leave immediately after the tenancy agreement is signed when the tenants move in. (If you do it on the same day, it is worth noting the *actual* time of agreement and notice so that it is clearly at a time after the agreement started.) It's easiest to do it then as most tenants will be happy to sign and it saves you having to make another visit. After four months, send your tenants a reminder that they have already been issued with a notice to leave as they may have forgotten.

If both parties agree to extend after the fixed term ends, you don't need to do anything special apart from getting your tenant to confirm in writing that he wishes to stay on. Later, when you want him to leave, it is best to give at least two months' notice and this notice must be dated to expire "after the last day of the tenancy". So, in the example above, the period of the tenancy is from the first to the thirtieth day of each month. Therefore, if you give notice on 10 August, the period of notice wouldn't actually start until 1 September and would end "after 30 October".

If there was no fixed term in the first place, then the

period of notice must still be two months but again it must state that it ends *after the last day of a "period" of a tenancy*. If, after the end of the fixed term, it's the tenant who wants to leave, he should give you at least a month's notice. Make sure you write the period of notice you require him to give you in the tenancy agreement.

The form of notice given to assured shorthold tenants requesting they leave is sometimes called a "Section 21 notice". Giving notice is important because, if you don't, you won't normally get a possession order in the unlikely event they don't leave and you end up needing to evict through the courts. (For more on evicting see Chapter 9, page 202.)

There is no need to pay a solicitor a fortune to draft a formal Section 21 notice for you. You can obtain a blank one from Oyez Stationers (see Appendix 2), your landlords' association or just draft a simple letter yourself.

If you compile your own letter, all you need is to make clear that you require the property back "after the appropriate date", giving the correct period of notice and stating that you require it back under Section 21 of the 1988 Housing Act. You need to include your name and address, the tenant's name and address and to refer to the property in question specifically. The letter must be dated and it's important to keep a record of the date and time of giving the notice and the method used – e.g. posting it or putting it through the letter-box. You could email a copy of the notice too. Keep copies of all correspondence.

The formal Section 21 notice has a lot of legalese, including a bit which basically tells the tenants that if they don't go, you have to apply to the court for a possession order. It's best to include this too.

Problems can arise when it's not certain if a tenant has

How to deliver a notice letter

Don't use recorded delivery to issue a notice, because if the tenant isn't in or refuses to sign, the letter won't be delivered. Use normal post and get a proof of posting certificate or hand deliver with an independent witness to verify it was delivered. Add extra days if the notice is sent by post as the two months' notice starts from the day the notice letter arrives.

---

left because you could end up being charged with unlawful eviction. Normally, you'll be on safe ground if the fixed term has ended and the tenant's possessions have gone, especially if the keys have been left at the property.

In the unlikely event that rent is in arrears, the tenant isn't contactable but his belongings are still at the property, it's best to get a possession order through the courts. For more on doing this, see Chapter 9. Meanwhile, try and make every effort to contact the tenant. If you have a telephone number or email address for friends, parents or work, try these.

Other things to do to make sure the end of tenancy goes smoothly

Lots of landlords and tenants who have otherwise had a perfectly good relationship end up falling out at the end of the tenancy over the return of the deposit. This is a shame because, with a bit of planning and hand holding, you and your tenants can remain on good terms.

The problem is that at the end of the tenancy most tenants don't know what they've got to do to get their deposit back. If they bothered to read the tenancy agreement and returned the property in the same state as when they let it, they would (or should) get all their deposit back. Unfortunately, many just file the agreement away and forget the state and condition of the property when they first moved in. I'm pleased to say I've never fallen out with a tenant over deposit money because I have a good system in place. Here's what I do.

When a tenant gives notice to leave, I first ask him to confirm it in writing. Once I have his confirmation letter, I then send him the letter on page 187. Often, there will be something that the tenant hasn't told you about before because it was too minor. Now is the time to find out and fix it ready for the new viewings.

Sample letter prior to leaving

Dear **NAME OF TENANT**
I acknowledge receipt of your letter and I'm sorry you are leaving. Leaving date is **INSERT DATE/TIME**. You must continue to pay rent up to the leaving date and under no circumstances use the deposit in lieu of the last month's rent.

If you should wish to move before this date, please call me as I sometimes have people who like the property and may want to move in earlier. If this should be the case, it might be possible to close the tenancy earlier.

Please note the following approximate times when I propose doing viewings with prospective new tenants: **INSERT TIMES AND DATES**. I'd be grateful if you can keep the house as tidy as possible at these times. Occasionally I may have someone who wishes to view at another time. If so, I will call you first to let you know and see if that time is convenient for you. I will accompany all viewings.

Please let me know if you are aware of anything in the property that needs repairing.

Finally, please read the "Important Notes" carefully. These notes simply highlight items in the Tenancy Agreement or relate to things that you need to do before you leave the property. If you have any questions or are unsure about anything explained here, please contact me as soon as possible.

If all is well, I'll be happy to provide a good reference. I will send further communication prior to the leaving date so watch out for this.
Yours sincerely

David Lawrenson

Important Notes
Please ensure that you have done the following:
1. That all the keys are returned.
2. That the property, including the garden, is returned in the same state at the end of the tenancy as it was at the start and after all your personal items have been removed. A deduction will be made from the deposit to repair and/or replace any damaged items or make

good any damaged property, fixtures, fittings, furniture and effects. (Fair wear and tear excepted.) Please take care not to damage walls when removing your own furniture! It is recommended that you use a properly qualified removal firm.

3. That all items in the inventory list are left in the same positions as they were at the start of the letting. The position of each item is listed in the Agreement under the section headed "Inventory". Any items that have been stored off-site must be returned.

In addition, I kindly request that you:

4. Provide all gas, electric, telephone, council tax and/or any other utility suppliers with a final meter reading and your forwarding address.
5. Provide me with a forwarding address and contact phone number.
6. Forward your post via the Royal Mail redirection service.
7. Arrange with the council for any bulky rubbish you no longer require to be collected before you move out.
8. Remove vehicles from the allocated parking bay.
9. Replace dead light bulbs.
10. Arrange to have the carpets professionally cleaned.

Note on cleaning
For cleaning, you should pay attention to the following:

• Cleaning outside and inside all cupboards, including kitchen cupboards.

- Removal of all stains and fat marks in the kitchen area (including on top of the kitchen units).
- Cleaning kitchen floor.
- Cleaning oven and grill including trays and racks.
- Cleaning bathroom area including removal of scale from taps and bath/shower fittings, inside and outside pan in WC/toilet and around rim of toilet.
- Cleaning and dusting including windows, window sills (inside and out), around and inside all light fittings, skirting boards, dado and picture rails. All surfaces.
- Defrosting and cleaning of fridge-freezer.
- Wiping down doors, door frames including street door and all woodwork.

Please note this is a guide, not an exhaustive list. If property is not cleaned to the state as was recorded and agreed in the inventory at the start of your tenancy agreement, additional cleaning that is required to be performed/arranged by the landlord will be charged and deducted from the deposit.

During the last few weeks of the old tenancy, I do a formal visit to see that everything works as it should. I check the oven, the shower, the central heating and whether the windows open properly. I test and check every item on the inventory including the beds, sofas and wardrobes. If things have been damaged I obtain two quotes and send these to the tenant with an explanation that this amount will be deducted from the deposit.

I may also go to the property a few days before the leaving date to check if the cleaning has started and to deal with any final questions the departing tenant has. On the leaving day, I meet with the tenant and check the inventory with him together with the inventory clerk. In case of dispute, I take along photos or a video showing the condition of the property when he moved in and check and agree meter readings for electricity, gas and water. If you can use the same *independent* inventory clerk who did the inventory and schedule of condition on move in, so much the better. It will seriously reduce the chances of a dispute.

Check everything thoroughly

After one tenant had left at the end of his tenancy, I made a cup of tea and sat down on one of the beds. It promptly collapsed! I checked the other bed – the same thing happened. Ditto the wardrobes! The tenant had obviously dismantled all the furniture to replace it with his own, and found it wouldn't go back together easily. Unfortunately I hadn't checked the furniture before he had left with his deposit. I had to pay a carpenter to put everything back together with extra supports. So, I now check all furniture when a tenant leaves and have inserted a clause in my agreement saying tenants must not dismantle any furniture.

If all is well, I return deposits (less any costs) on the leaving date itself when the tenant hands over the keys. Some tenants ask for it in cash, which I'd avoid, but if you must do this, make sure you get them to sign for it and have their signature witnessed.

If you hold the deposit, you should not hold onto it for more than ten days after the end of the tenancy. The only possible time I might hold onto the deposit for a couple of days is if the rent is paid directly to me by the housing benefit office. If so, I check with the housing benefit people that it's all up-to-date and they have made no overpayment. (The rules on payment of housing benefit are constantly changing, but you may be justified in holding onto some deposit money for a few days in case the housing benefit authorities later try to claw it back from you.)

It's worth noting that once final utility meter readings and a forwarding address have been taken by you in good faith, the council tax authority and utility suppliers can't come after you for money owed to them by your tenants. So, again, you've no reason to hold any of their deposit pending final bills.

I usually allow a few days between the old tenants leaving and the new ones moving in, in case anything needs fixing or if the previous tenants have not cleaned up properly.

If you do all this, or check that your agent is doing it, you'll never have an argument with your tenant about the return of his deposit. If you part on good company, ask your old tenants if they would be happy to provide references on you, the landlord, for other prospective tenants! Many will be delighted to do this and only too pleased to tell people what a good landlord you have been.

Respecting your tenants' privacy
When planning viewings with prospective tenants, I always fix a few specific times during the week and stick to them. Only if I have someone who sounds really good, and who can't make one of these times, will I call my tenant to make an appointment for another time. That way, I respect my existing tenants' privacy. It's worth including a clause in your agreement allowing you to do viewings with prospective tenants in the last month of the tenancy.

When the property is vacant between tenants I always ensure it's properly locked and secured. I leave a few lights and a radio on a timer switch to give the impression someone is in. It's best to visit regularly and pick up the post, especially if it is left in a public area like a communal hallway. Don't allow a "To Let" board as it's a dead give-away the place is empty.

Squatters look for empty properties where an agent's board is outside, post is piling up and there aren't any lights on. There are websites out there telling squatters to look for just these kinds of unsecured houses. You've been warned! If you leave a window open and they get in without using force, you'll have a lot of hassle getting rid of them.

Tenancy deposit schemes

Things have changed in the way landlords have to handle deposits. All landlords in England and Wales who take deposits on new assured shorthold tenancies from 6 April 2007 have to join government-approved tenancy deposit schemes (TDS) which have the aim of protecting tenants' deposits. The schemes (run for the Government by private approved organisations) have dispute resolution procedures in place for landlords and tenants who can't agree about the deposit at the end of the tenancy.

The new rules were brought in to try to make it easier for tenants to reclaim their deposits at the end of the tenancy since it was felt that many landlords were unfairly holding onto them. The Government had obviously forgotten that it already had a perfectly good scheme called the small claims court available for use but it introduced these new schemes anyway – and a whole additional layer of bureaucracy!

There are two types of TDS: a "custodial" scheme where a third party holds the deposit; and an "insurance" scheme where the landlord holds it. Landlords have to tell tenants which scheme they are in and provide full details of how the scheme works within fourteen days of receiving the deposit. (The schemes have downloadable documents and certificates of deposit protection that can be sent to the tenant.) If landlords don't do this, penalties include having to pay the tenant an amount of three times the deposit and becoming ineligible to regain possession under the so-called "accelerated possession procedure".

The insurance scheme seems to be the better option as it is relatively cheap and allows landlords to hold onto their deposits rather than paying them to a third party. The only downside of the insurance schemes is that landlords have to pay a small fee to join and for each deposit taken. With the insurance based schemes, only if at the end of the tenancy is there a dispute must the landlord lodge the disputed amount with the scheme until the dispute is resolved – with the rest being returned to the tenant within ten days. If, for any reason, the landlord does not pay into the scheme, the administrators will return the disputed amount to the tenant (if they are entitled to it) and chase the landlord for recovery of the money. The landlord and tenant can opt out of the schemes' free dispute resolution service, if they wish, and go to court instead.

There is just one custodial scheme, run by Computershare Services Plc at www.depositprotection.com. It is free but uses the interest on landlords' deposits to pay for the admin.

There are two insurance-based schemes. One is run by Tenancy Deposit Solutions (www.mydeposits.co.uk) and is mainly aimed at landlords; the other is run by the Dispute Service Ltd (www.thedisputeservice.co.uk) and is mainly targeted at agents, though both landlords and agents are free to join either scheme.

Note that the scheme only covers *new agreements* from 6 April 2007. So, if you have an existing tenancy agreement that started before that date, you can avoid having to join a deposit protection scheme by simply extending the existing agreement so it becomes a monthly periodic tenancy.

The new schemes do add extra work and cost for landlords – and the administrative requirements of the schemes are, in my opinion, unnecessarily detailed, but once you have done it a few times it gets easier.

Landlords should note that the very existence of the

schemes makes it all the more important to appoint an independent inventory clerk to do a thorough inventory with time dated photos, thus evidencing the state and condition of the property at the start and end of each tenancy.

You can avoid TDS completely by issuing an assured tenancy instead of an assured shorthold one, but if you do this you will not be able to regain possession unless the tenant seriously breached the tenancy agreement or the tenant left voluntarily. I would advise against doing this.

Currently, plans for introducing the scheme in Scotland and Northern Ireland are being considered. Watch this space!

How to manage utilities and council tax

In between lettings you'll have to pay the utilities and, if the property is furnished, the council tax. For utilities, keep a note of start and end readings and supply the tenant's forwarding address for bills. It's worth keeping a record of all conversations because I once had the council tax people incorrectly sending bills to me at my rented property instead of my correspondence address. The tenant forgot to send me the bill and I nearly ended up in court for non-payment! Luckily I had a record of the phone call where I gave the council my correspondence address.

I now put in my tenancy agreements that tenants must forward any post addressed to me personally or to "the owner" as soon as possible. Post addressed to the "occupier" must be opened by them and passed on to me if it's relevant for me to see it – for example, if it is related to construction work or a planning application nearby.

In the agreement I also advise tenants that I'll pass on the names and forwarding addresses of *each* tenant to utility companies and the council tax people when they move in and leave. Council taxpayers living on their own are entitled to a discount so if you have more than one person renting your property, tell them not to try to cheat the council by pretending they're living alone when they aren't.

Tenants are free to change their utility supplier as they see fit.

How to manage paperwork

One thing that soon becomes apparent to new landlords is that there is a lot of paperwork to deal with. As well as the usual bills to pay for each property, there are also tenancy agreements, inventory/condition lists, invoices and mortgage statements to file.

It's also useful to keep your own record of where the stop valves/fuse boxes are, how the heating system works, room sizes, the location of the meters, parking space, communal bins and any other useful information on the property. Keep a diary log for each property to record notes of any conversation or phone calls with tenants, agents, even the meter readings given to the water company! I keep leftovers and samples of the types of carpet and paint used in each room for when I need to replace it.

If you have a flat you'll be a leaseholder or you may own the freehold on your own or with others. The lease contract sets out who should do what in relation to the property and the various rights and obligations on each side. Keep a record in your diary log of all events, phone calls and copies of all correspondence with other lease-holders, the freeholder and managing agent. See the section in Chapter 3 on Freehold or Leasehold.

You need an up-to-date filing system for all this and to keep invoices and statements for up to six years to satisfy the Revenue. I file my records by property and my rents and invoices in date order. These can then be re-sorted by property, supplier or type of bill. Sorting by bill type makes it easier to complete your tax return because HMRC requires that costs be grouped into different categories. For more on reporting for tax purposes, see Chapter 11.

You can buy software, where if you enter information in, say, an invoice file, it will automatically fill in another form which can be sent to the Revenue or update a management report. It's worth looking into these especially if you have a lot of properties.

How to keep up-to-date
The law on letting property and the requirements made of you as a landlord change from time to time so you need to keep up-to-date. The property pages of the national newspapers are a good source for finding out about changes and, if you use a good letting agency, they should be able to keep you up-to-date too. Make sure to ask them though because keeping you informed won't be their top priority!

Better still, join a landlords' association. They offer a way to meet other landlords, receive information and updates and use free helplines. Of course, there is also my own site, www.LettingFocus.com which also has a useful and regularly updated blog. Finally, there is the occasional property show you can attend. These have lots of useful seminars you can go to for a small fee. Be careful, though, estate agents and property syndicates occupy about 80 per cent of the stands at these shows. They are all hungry for your money, so leave your chequebook at home!

One last thing, if you are a member of a landlords' association (or are accredited with your local authority) you may get a discount on the cost of your licence application if you have a licensable HMO and on the cost of things like Energy Performance Certificates and tenancy deposit schemes. To find out if your local authority runs an accreditation scheme for private landlords ask your council's housing department or check their website.

9

DIFFICULT TENANTS AND HOW TO DEAL WITH THEM

The vast majority of tenants are good and there are only a few bad ones who could cost you a fortune. The good news is that provided you reference your tenant properly (see Chapter 7) then it's very unlikely you'll end up with a bad one. However, I can't stress enough that it's essential to ask for and check references thoroughly and never let a tenant in until all checks have been done and both deposit and rent have been paid – in cash.

Many landlords get their tenant from hell through a letting agent, so if you use an agent I'm afraid you must still check the references yourself. It's just too important to trust someone else to do this for you.

The sorts of things that can go wrong . . . and how to deal with them
Things that can go wrong with tenants boil down to one or more of the following:

• They don't look after the property properly.

- They annoy the neighbours.
- They don't pay the rent.
- They don't move out when they're supposed to.

If they don't look after the property or they annoy the neighbours but are paying the rent, then you just need to change their behaviour. In these cases, it's often that they are young people away from home for the first time. They simply need to be put on the right track!

For example, if they've painted a bedroom black, you need to explain that they must put it back to the original colour before the end of the tenancy. If they allowed an obvious water leak to continue, tell them they may be liable for the cost of repairing the resultant damage. If they annoy neighbours with loud music, explain that other people have to get up for work in the morning! If they've broken something, tell them they'll be liable for the cost of repair.

If they are students with parent guarantors tell the guarantor about the problem. Parents usually come down heavily on wayward offspring if they're behaving unreasonably. Go through the tenancy agreement and House Guide again and remind your tenants of their responsibilities to look after the property.

Ask if there is anything you can do to help. If the garden is a mess, do they have tools to keep it in good order? If not, get some. If damp has built up, did you impress on them the importance of opening windows regularly? Could they do with a clothes line to dry things outside? If they just live in a mess then that's not your business, though you should make it clear that the property must be left clean and tidy at the end of the tenancy.

If the rent doesn't show up in your account, it might be that they have just genuinely forgotten, in which case a polite phone call and written reminder will do the trick.

Sometimes you need to be flexible. Suppose you have someone who has rented from you for a year and he contacts you to say he has lost his job so the rent will be two weeks late. In this case, I'd agree to the delay but I'd get him to commit to the exact date the rent would be in my account and make it clear that I would not allow any further delays.

Where a person loses his job, he may be entitled to housing benefit or local housing allowance. However, it's usually paid four weeks in arrears and tends to be (though is not always) less than the full rent. If you accept payment through the housing benefit system, you are advised to do all you can to help the tenant with the claim. Offer to take the tenant to the housing benefit office and help with his application, monitor the claim progress carefully and if there are arrears apply to get the benefit paid to you directly. If you can't wait for the housing benefit to come through, you may need to give notice to leave. Whilst you can be sympathetic, you must remember this is a business. You don't have a duty to house people who can't afford to pay and the failings of the benefit system aren't your problem! Your tenants can always move somewhere smaller and cheaper.

If it's mid way through a fixed term contract, you're better off letting the tenants leave early as there is no point insisting they pay until the end. Point them towards a good source of other lettings and say that, if they go early and you don't incur actual losses, you'll still give them a good reference.

If a tenant's rent is late, he makes no effort to contact

you and avoids you when you call, then you may have a bigger problem. He may have no intention of paying – either because he can't or he would rather spend the rent on other things. Again, you should give him an option to leave early but you may have to take legal action to evict him through the courts.

What if a tenant doesn't move out when he is supposed to? If a tenant pays the rent on time but doesn't move out when he should, this will usually be due to a misunderstanding. Sometimes it happens that the property that he was moving to has fallen through and he needs to stay just a few more weeks. Try to be as flexible as circumstances allow!

How to evict a tenant
In this section, unless stated otherwise, I shall cover the situation as far as Assured Tenancies (including Assured Shorthold Tenancies) are concerned in England and Wales. For a guide to the different kinds of tenancy see Chapter 6.

When evicting tenants, you need to have a "ground" for eviction and to have served a proper notice on the tenant before legal proceedings are started.

There are seventeen different grounds for eviction and these can be either "mandatory" or "discretionary". Where the ground is mandatory, provided that your paperwork is OK, the judge must grant an order for possession. With discretionary grounds it's up to the judge. Most landlords therefore use a mandatory ground. (If only discretionary grounds are claimed, the tenant may be able to get legal aid to help his defence, and you could have a big legal bill to pay if you lose. Public funding may also be available for mandatory grounds if the tenant's lawyers can identify a defence e.g. the initial notice was invalid, etc.)

The main mandatory grounds are:

- Where the fixed term has come to an end (called the shorthold ground).
- Where there are serious rent arrears (sometimes called ground 8).
- Where the landlord previously occupied the property (sometimes called ground 1).

Let's look at each a bit further.

Where the fixed term has come to an end
Where the fixed term has come to an end and you have given at least two months' notice to quit in the form called a section 21 notice, you will automatically get a possession order should it come to court. You cannot obtain possession under this ground during the first six months of the original tenancy.

A section 21 notice can also be served if the tenancy is periodic, i.e. running from month to month. Where the tenancy is periodic or the notice is served after the expiry of the fixed term tenancy then the notice must expire on the last day of the period of the tenant's tenancy – the problem of accurately identifying the date can be avoided by giving the tenant notice that possession is required "at the end of the period of your tenancy which will end next after the expiration of two months from the service upon you of this notice". For more detailed advice on how to issue a section 21 notice at the end of the tenancy see Chapter 8, page 184.

Where there are serious rent arrears
Where there are rent arrears of at least two months' rent (in the case of a monthly paid tenancy) when you serve

notice (a section 8 notice), you will always be granted possession at the date of any subsequent court hearing. If the rent is payable weekly, quarterly or yearly this ground requires rent arrears of eight weeks, three months and six months respectively.

The section 8 and section 21 notices are easy to complete and can be obtained from legal stationers like Oyez (see Appendix 2) or landlords' associations. If you serve a section 8 notice for serious rent arrears, you must give the tenant two weeks' notice that you want possession. If he doesn't leave, you then go to court to seek a judgment in your favour.

If you use this ground, claim at the same time under the discretionary grounds for general rent arrears (ground 10) and persistent late payment (ground 11) so you can get a judgment for rent arrears owed too.

If the property was previously occupied by you
If you occupied the property before the tenancy started and wish to occupy it again (or if it was previously a holiday let), you need to give written notice to the tenant before the tenancy starts that possession may be granted on this ground. Then, when you need the property again, give the tenant a section 8 notice at least two months before you want possession. If he doesn't go, you would then go to court and be automatically granted possession. Again, it's worth claiming under grounds 10 and 11 too.

How to serve a notice
The service of the correct form of notice in writing must be done before you can get a possession order. If you can't prove that you have done this, you will not usually obtain your possession order. The correct notice to be served will

depend upon the ground you are using and whether or not the fixed term has expired.

Keep a record of the date and time and method of how the notice was served. Ideally it's best to deliver it through the tenant's letter-box yourself, preferably with a witness, so the tenant cannot say it got lost in the post or get a proof of posting certificate from the post office. Don't use recorded delivery as the tenant can refuse to accept it.

Section 8 notices remain valid for one year so you can start court action to evict at any time until twelve months after the date the notice expires. If, for some reason, you don't start court action within this time you'd have to send a new notice. For section 21 notices, there is no validity period, but the landlord must act consistently with his requirement that the tenant vacate at the expiry of the notice. So proceed quickly!

Possession proceedings
The court procedure for evicting a tenant who won't go or who owes you rent is relatively simple and you follow a straightforward county court process. You'll need to fill in a few forms, which you can do yourself without a lawyer. The staff at the court can help and will check your documents for you, though they can't offer legal advice.

Two types of court proceedings are available: "normal" and so called "accelerated" possession proceedings.

Accelerated possession
Accelerated possession can only be used if you're claiming on the shorthold ground – i.e. because the tenant hasn't moved out after the end of the fixed term and a valid section 21 notice has been served and expired. You can't use accelerated possession to claim arrears of rent.

Evidence is presented in writing so you don't have to go to a court hearing. Once the court has issued papers to the tenant, he has fourteen days to reply after which an order for possession will be made and the tenant told to leave within fourteen days. Although you'll have to pay the fairly modest court fee upfront, the order will be made for the loser, in this case the tenant, to pay this cost.

The court judgment will be against anyone in your property at the time. So, if your tenant has decided to sublet your property to another unsuspecting third party (as my problem tenant once did) then that third party also has to go on that date. If the third party has been a victim of fraud by your tenant, that's tough; he still has to leave. The possession order gives a date for possession. If on that date the tenants or anyone else is still there, you'll have to fill in another form and send another fee to the court for them to appoint a bailiff. This will add on another three to five weeks depending on the court. Are you beginning to see the importance of checking references carefully at the outset?

Please note, even when you have a possession order, you can't make the tenants leave yourself. You need a court bailiff to do this. When the bailiff goes in, you need to be there to take possession formally. You'll also need a locksmith in attendance to change the locks.

Normal possession

"Normal proceedings" is the name for the court process used for all types of possession other than accelerated possession. Normal proceedings will involve a court hearing which you'll have to attend. You will normally get a money judgment for arrears due and an order that the tenant pays you until he leaves. If the tenant doesn't pay up, you'll have to fill in some more papers at court and another small fee to "enforce the judgment".

However, before you embark on trying to get money out of a tenant through the courts, you need to decide if you're ever going to get it back anyway. If not, and if it's near to the end of the fixed term, you might be best waiting and going down the accelerated possession route to get him out.

There is much useful guidance to help with pursuing possession procedures in material published by the Court Service (see Appendix 2) and from landlords' associations. Again, court staff will usually help and show you what forms you need and how to complete them. You'll also get excellent advice if you join a landlords' association; their helplines are staffed by fellow landlords who have been there before and can give good free advice as well as offer sympathy.

Using a solicitor
If you feel you really must use a solicitor, use one experienced in landlord and tenant work and get a firm quotation upfront. Get him to agree to a fixed price for the eviction and not just working unspecified hours at an hourly rate.

How to make a claim for money owed

Occasionally, you might want to make a claim for money you are owed but without the need to claim possession. It might be that the tenant has already left the property owing money or that the condition of the vacated property will cost more to put right than the amount of deposit.

Where money claims are for small amounts, currently under £5,000, they are dealt with by what is called the "small claims procedure" in the county court. Again, you simply get the forms from the court and complete them yourself following the easy to read leaflets. If you are claiming damages, obtain a couple of estimates for the cost of the work and submit any documentary proof (e.g. photographs) to back up your claim. You also need to provide a copy of the tenancy agreement and any rent books. Only if the claim is defended will you have to go to a hearing. There is a small court fee to pay.

Occasionally, landlords have to defend claims where the tenant is seeking return of his deposit, which perhaps was withheld due to damage. If so, you'll need evidence to back up why the deposit is being withheld.

Most money claims aren't defended by tenants. If you win, the tenant will be told to pay you and the court fee too. You'll then have to hope the tenant actually pays up. Many don't, which means that you'll have to go to court again to get them to enforce the judgment. However, if the tenant has left you'll have to find him to get payment due to you and this may involve employing a tracing service/debt collector.

If the tenant has no money, it may be a long time before you are repaid (if at all). Sometimes the tenant will counterclaim, in which case it will probably be decided at a court hearing.

Despite the problem of actually getting your money back through the courts, I would urge all landlords who are owed money at least to sue in the small claims court and get a judgment against the tenant, even if you can't be bothered actually to enforce the judgment. The court fee is small and it will at least make it more difficult for the tenant to get credit or to rip off another landlord, as it will show up under his name at that address as a County Court Judgment (CCJ). You can see it as your duty to other landlords and will be at least some form of retribution!

Some useful tips

If you're taking someone to court for non-payment, don't discuss the matter with him. Provided that you did all you could to get in contact with him beforehand, there is nothing left to say. Don't listen to sob stories; remember it's not personal it's just business. Your only reason to stop a court order would be if he pays up all that is owed immediately, which means in cash today. You should accept nothing less because once you stop a court order, that's it – you'd have to start the whole thing off again from the beginning.

Ensure that there are no grounds that the tenant can counter-claim on, such as repairs not being done.

For some claims you can use the courts online claims service.

Not many landlords know this, but for tenancies that started before December 2003 the tenancy documents should be stamped. Stamp duty of £5 is payable on most tenancies where the rent for the term is over £5,000. Most landlords don't bother unless there is a risk that the tenancy document may be produced in court, which it will if possession proceedings start. Although documents should be stamped within thirty days of execution, the Stamp Office generally accept late documents on payment of a small penalty charge.

In fact, the possibility that a tenant may have a CCJ is the main reason why it's important to perform a credit reference check against each tenant's name at his previous addresses. If he is reluctant to give you evidence of previous addresses and/or a reference from his last landlord, it might be that he is hiding a County Court Judgment. In these cases, you should be very wary of letting to him. You have been warned!

Many tenants will pay up at the threat of court action. They know the problems they'll have with a CCJ against their name. Some, unfortunately, are too far gone to care or are going abroad where their poor UK credit reference will not affect them.

Evicting squatters and Rent Act tenants

In law there is no legal definition of a squatter, just a trespasser. If a trespasser is in occupation you can rely on self-help measures (i.e. not involving the court) to get the property back. Clearly, what you will have to do is somehow get into the property and change the locks and secure it. But although you can do it yourself – and you would be wise to have the police there when the squatters come back – what you cannot do is use violent entry if one of the squatters is actually in the property at the time and opposes you.

Of course, clued-up squatters know this, so they change the locks and always make sure that someone is in the property – not hard for them as most won't have jobs. They will no doubt quote the relevant law – which is section 6 of the Criminal Law Act 1977 – and call the police and friendly lawyers to stop you from trying to evict them.

So to counter this you will need to use the special

court process for trespassers. Usually these can be issued quickly – often in less than four weeks. For most people this will be the most attractive option and is usually easier than waiting in vain for them to go out before you can go in and change the locks. It is also much better from the point of view of your own physical safety.

The good thing about going to court is that the squatters will almost certainly go just before the bailiffs arrive, taking their stuff (or at least the stuff they want to take!) with them.

If the property was your former home, or was somewhere that you were about to move into, then you have a right to get back in as a Protected Intending Occupier (PIO) under section 7 of the 1977 Act. You will need to prove that it was your former home or that you have recently bought it and intended to move into it – which you can do by getting a written statement and having it witnessed by a solicitor. You then go to the police and request their assistance with gaining re-entry and effecting the removal of the squatters.

You can also use this approach if the squatters had got in while the property was empty between tenants and you have already got a tenancy agreement with new tenants.

Of course, actually getting the police to assist may be hard work, so you may decide to opt for the special court procedures anyway.

If your tenant lets the squatters in (and assuming you did not allow your tenant to sublet to them), it gets a bit more complicated. In this case it's probably best to be safe and pursue the normal track possession route through the courts to get possession. (In other words, you would still in effect have to assume that your tenant was in possession!) In this case, your possession order is in effect made "against the world" – meaning against anyone who happens to be in your property, irrespective of whether they are mentioned in court papers or not!

To avoid people just letting themselves into your property and becoming squatters, keep your property secured at all times, especially between tenancies and before the completion of the conveyancing.

Windows should not be left open because with no evidence of forced entry, squatters cannot be treated as burglars.

Dealing with squatters and Rent Act tenants is complex so I would strongly advise you to seek legal advice from a solicitor experienced in dealing with these issues.

Whatever you do, don't harass!
By now you're probably thinking the law is a bit of an ass to allow a former tenant to stay in your property rent-free for three to five months while the legal process drags to its slow conclusion and you finally get your property back. Well, if it's any consolation, thousands of other landlords agree with you. That's why it's so important to be very careful with reference checks. Tight checks (and a deposit of at least five weeks) will put off bad tenants. They'll seek an easier sucker elsewhere.

Landlords who suffer from bad tenants experience a feeling of anger, rage and impotence that someone can effectively steal from them in this way. Not only is there the lost rent, but you'll incur about £200 court costs if it has to go all the way to a bailiff eviction, much more if you employ a solicitor. And a bad tenant is bad through and through. As well as spending time filling in court forms, you'll have to change locks, clean up after the tenant, deal with sending back all his other unpaid bills and possibly angry neighbours too.

The anger is all the more acute when the tenant clearly has money but chooses to spend it on other things. In some cases, tenants even insist you do repairs, despite having not paid rent! They may also run illegal activities from the property. Faced with this kind of professional tenant conman, many landlords are tempted to get heavy, use threatening behaviour, try to evict the tenant themselves, enter the property without consent, change the locks or cut off the tenant's electricity.

However bad the tenants are, you must always follow the correct legal procedures, even though it takes time. If you resort to "self-help" measures, you have a very good chance of facing criminal or civil action. Naturally, any civil action from the tenant will probably be financed by legal aid so, if you lose, you'll have to pay not only damages but legal costs too. Landlords who don't know the law are sitting ducks for rapacious no-win no-fee solicitors. So, be careful.

What to do if a tenant dies
It's rare but it can happen that a tenant can die whilst renting your property. If you've referenced the tenant, you should be able to get in touch with his employer or his next of kin fairly quickly. If it's a joint tenancy, the other tenant(s) would remain responsible for the rent.

You can hold the tenant's estate liable to pay the rent until the end of any fixed term, although in my opinion this is a bit unethical. However, it would be reasonable to expect to recover any expenses you incur out of the rent that was due. This would include any costs incurred for storage and cleaning.

How to solve housing benefit/ local housing allowance problems

If your tenant is on housing benefit, and if the rent is also paid direct to you, the council may ask you to repay it if, for example, the tenant was caught working and wasn't entitled to the benefit. If this happens, write to the council asking for the exact reason for the overpayment. Then ask for a review of the decision, putting all the blame on the tenant's failure to notify a change of circumstances. If this fails to satisfy them, you are entitled to have an independent appeal tribunal decide the matter.

As a pre-emptive step, make regular visits to the property to ensure that any such tenant's circumstances haven't changed – e.g. he has got a job or moved someone in. If they have changed, tell the housing benefit officer. For advice on how to speed up payment of housing benefit see Chapter 7, page 161.

Questions and answers

Q. My tenant is behind on his rent? What do I do?

A. It depends how long the arrears are. You have to wait until he is two months in arrears as the judge is then obliged to make a possession order. Then, send the tenant a section 8 notice citing grounds 8, 10 and 11 and stating you require possession in fourteen days' time. If he doesn't go, go to the county court and ask for the appropriate forms to complete. A hearing will take place about four to eight weeks later which you must attend.

Q. I have had complaints that my tenant is running a brothel from the house he rents from me.

A. Send the tenant a special section 8 notice quoting ground 14 with just one day's notice. Proceedings can be commenced immediately the notice has been served. Ask at the county court for the appropriate forms to complete.

Q. I issued a section 21 notice and the tenants have not left. Can I kick the tenants out?

A. No, the tenants don't have to leave until evicted by the bailiffs. Your next course of action would be to ask at the county court for the forms for Accelerated Possession.

Q. My tenants owed me over two months' rent so I went to court and got a possession order giving the tenants fourteen days to leave. However, they are still there. What can be done?

A. Obtain from the court the appropriate form to instruct the bailiffs.

Q. I bought a house with some "Assured Tenants" in it. They don't have a written tenancy agreement. Will this be a problem?

A. If the tenants were there before 28 February 1997, they will be "assured" tenants unless you specified other-wise. You don't strictly need a written tenancy agreement to have a tenancy. However, if they are not assured shorthold tenants and there is a problem, you won't be able to use the Accelerated Possession procedure. In order to evict, you would need to prove a serious breach of the tenancy and attend a hearing

Q. The annual gas inspection is due, but the tenant won't let my gas engineer in. What can I do?

A. Write to the tenant and explain that it's a legal requirement (under section 11(6) of the Landlord and Tenant Act 1985) for the landlord to obtain access to the property at reasonable times of the day on twenty-four hours' written notice for the purpose of viewing the condition and state of repair. Keep copies of all correspondence and a diary log to record visits and phone calls, in case of dispute later.

Q. My tenant has left owing me money and I don't know where he has gone. I know he has money so I could make a claim against him. But how do I find him?

A. Consider employing the services of a tracing agent. Contact the Credit Services Association (0191 286 5656, www.csa-uk.com) or the Association of British Investigators (www.theabi.org.uk).

Q Can I make a possession claim online?

A Yes you can and it can be faster. Go to https://www.possessionclaim.gov.uk/pcol

10

WHEN IT'S TIME TO SELL

Professional landlords are always evaluating their property investments against other properties (and other investments) elsewhere. So should you. If the property has gone up in price but the rent has stayed the same, then it might be worth thinking about selling and investing instead in another area or type of property with better yields or better growth prospects.

When thinking about selling it's important not to forget to include all the legal costs as well as the cost of any agent involved in the sale. Also budget for any costs needed to smarten up the property for sale as well as any period when the property is empty and no rent is coming in. Include transaction costs for any new property in your evaluation too. Finally don't forget about possible capital gains tax implications too. See Chapter 11 for more on this.

Anyway, when it's time to sell, you'll want to get the best price as quickly as you can. This short chapter provides some help and advice about selling a property.

What's the best time of year to sell?

If you can pick the ideal time of year to sell, the best time to get property on the market is late February. The market starts to hot up with lots of buyers through late February and into March, April and early summer. It tends to die off in high summer, picks up a bit in September and October and dies the death by November and December.

How to sell successfully through an estate agent

Selling through an agent is a tried and tested way of getting a sale. Estate agency fees for selling vary depending on the state of the market, the type of property and how hard they think it will be to sell it. Typically they vary from 1 to 3 per cent. Negotiate as hard as you can and get valuations from at least three agents. Look for the following:

- The agent should guarantee to advertise in local newspapers. (Lots of buyers only look at the local press property ads.)
- They should be able to provide evidence that they have sold lots of properties like yours. It's worth checking what kind of properties they sell, because some agents will be too up-market or down-market for your type of property.
- They should have a good website and advertise on the major portals such as RightMove or Primelocation.com.
- Their office should be in a busy, prominent and accessible location. If they have more than one office, they should actively sell your property from their other offices too.
- Their "For Sale" boards should be attractive and eye-catching.

- They should be prepared to explain how their valuation was arrived at.
- They should have good staff. Not just the manager but all staff, including weekend ones, should be professional, efficient and easy to get on with.
- They should be prepared to negotiate on their fee and should consider performance related fees linked to the sale price achieved. There should be no additional fees for any special marketing they do for you.
- They should take care in producing accurate property details that present your property in the best light for potential buyers. (Floor plans and colour photos are plus points here!)
- They should open on Saturdays.
- They should give you feedback following viewings.
- They should properly "qualify" potential buyers. (If you are concerned that a buyer is "flaky", ask the agent for sight of the mortgage offer. If there is no sign of a surveyor/mortgage offer within two weeks, insist that the property be remarketed. If it's a cash buyer, ask his bank to prove that he really has the funds.)
- They should keep you updated as the sale progresses.
- They should allow you to suggest improvements to their advertisement for the property.
- They should work quickly and efficiently.

Check your contract with the agent carefully. In particular:

- Don't sign a long contract with an agency, but give them at least a month so that they have a real chance of selling it.
- Sole agency is usually best unless you have a good reason to go for multiple agencies. If you must go multiple, avoid a cluster of For Sale boards outside as it

looks desperate. If you change agents, make sure the old board is removed from the property.

- Don't accept "sole selling rights" as this would mean you would have to pay them, even if you eventually sold it privately to a friend.
- Don't accept a clause whereby you still pay them fees if you withdraw after they've found you a buyer.
- Keep the property photo up-to-date. (If the photo was taken in high summer and it's now midwinter, it will be obvious that it has been on the market a long time.)

Don't give an agent or buyer too much information about your personal circumstances. If he knows that your tenants have gone and you are no longer getting income on it, he'll think you're more desperate to sell and will accept lower offers.

Do listen to feedback from viewers and the agent. If it's not selling because something basic needs fixing, then fix it. If it's a mess, tidy up! If the furnishing/presentation/paint colour is awful, get it sorted. Read the section in Chapter 5 about decorating for tenants as the tips explained there apply equally well if you are selling a property too. If all else fails, consider reducing the price.

Selling at auction

You don't need an estate agent to sell your property. Alternatives are selling at auction and selling it yourself. If you sell at auction, you will, at least, have serious buyers with the necessary deposit who can complete within a month. Auctions may be a particularly good idea if your property is run down or in any way unusual. Fees are roughly equivalent to sales through estate agents. However, you will probably get less than if you had sold through an agent.

Selling it yourself

Selling yourself can work too, though it can be time-consuming. You may be able to advertise in the local press, on your company website or on public notice boards in supermarkets and libraries for free. Try your landlords' organisation too. Other landlords might be interested in buying it as a going concern with your tenants in place and this will save you from having a void period before you sell it. Advertising to sell with tenants in place will of course work best where the tenants keep the property clean and tidy.

Home Information Pack (HIP)

Sellers should note that the requirement for vendors to have a Home Information Pack has now been withdrawn though they must provide an Energy Performance Certificate.

In Scotland, the whole conveyancing process is, of course, much easier and faster than in England and Wales. Here, the contract becomes legally binding much earlier. This stops people making multiple offers on different properties and minimises the risk of being gazumped. Also, since a formal moving date is set, it is much easier to co-ordinate sale and purchase, thereby removing some of the problems of being in a chain.

Think about the time of day that best shows off your property and do your viewings then. Allow potential buyers to walk into the room before you because, if you go first, you'll take up space and the property will seem smaller. If you market it yourself, keep an eye on your personal security: see Chapter 7, page 143.

Never say that the property is empty at any time or leave it unsecured. If it's empty, give the impression it's occupied by setting internal lights on timer switches. Also, think carefully before putting up a For Sale sign, especially if it's in a crime-ridden area – you could attract squatters or burglars.

Why it pays to be prepared

Don't give away too much information if you are desperate to sell. If an agent or potential buyer asks how long it's been on the market, answer vaguely; it's not on the list of questions that you must legally answer!

Negotiate coolly and be unemotional about it. Have all necessary information ready to answer positively any possible question – e.g. whether it's south-facing, when the windows were put in, the level of council tax, parks, transport, improvement plans for the area, good local school results, lack of crime, etc.

Speed up the sale process by having additional documents like insurance policies, warranties, guarantees, manuals and instructions available for the buyer. Use a local conveyancing firm to whom you can hand deliver/ pick up documents; this will avoid the "it's in the post" excuse beloved of solicitors.

11

TAX

Ah, you are probably thinking, here is a nasty, boring subject. Also, you might be worried it's a bit hard to understand. Well, the good news is that taxes on property are not too harsh. In fact, Her Majesty's Revenue and Customs (HMRC), or "The Revenue" as I will usually refer to them, is very kind to property investors. However, property tax is a teeny bit complicated, mainly because there are so many nooks and crannies within it, but understanding it means you can significantly reduce your tax bill.

I'll do my best to make it as simple and interesting as I can. However, you may need to read this chapter a bit more carefully and slowly than the other chapters in this book. So, relax, get a cup of coffee and take your time and you'll be well on the way to becoming an expert! Before we start I'll make it clear that for convenience I have used the term "couple" or "married couples" to refer to "legally married couples" and to same sex partners in civil partnerships – who have the same rights, of course.

First, two quick words of warning! The Revenue change

their rules often so check their website for the latest position (see Appendix 2) or give them a call and get their latest fact sheets. Also, to find what is best for your own circumstances seek advice from an accountant, tax adviser or specialist like Smith & Williamson (see Appendix 2). Check that whoever you employ is good at advising on property and get a fixed quote for what you want him to do.

Unfortunately, there are many different taxes that affect landlords (and this chapter is focused on advice for people who are primarily *landlords* rather than property developers or traders.)

Let's look at the various taxes.

When you buy a property, like anyone else you'll probably have to pay stamp duty land tax. When it's rented out, you may have to pay income tax. When you die, your estate may have to pay inheritance tax. If you set up a company and use this as a vehicle to buy your properties, your company may have to pay corporation tax. When

---

If you live abroad

If you are a non-UK resident, the situation may differ slightly from that explained here and you may also be taxed in your country of residence subject to any double taxation agreement the UK Government has set up with the country where you live. Check with the Revenue and your local tax authority. Non-residents using a letting agent for management should get an exemption from the Revenue so rent can be paid over to them gross by the agent (although they may still be required to complete a UK tax return). For the tax position on investment properties abroad, see Chapter 12, page 259.

you sell, you may have to pay capital gains tax. Whenever you buy goods and services, you'll have to pay VAT. Finally, if you have lots of properties and employ other people, then you'll have to pay employer's national insurance contributions.

However, the main taxes that matter significantly are capital gains tax and income tax so I'll focus mainly on these and touch on some of the others where relevant.

Completing the tax return

When you do your tax return, you have to write down your income and costs from property letting on the special supplementary pages for property. You can get these by calling the Revenue's helpline or downloading them from their website. The Revenue should then send you the pages every year automatically.

Completing the supplementary pages is easy. Simply follow the help sheets and list separately the income and costs from normal property lettings and furnished holiday accommodation. You will need to tick the "rent a room" box if applicable. Overseas lettings go on the foreign pages and capital gains go on the capital gains pages. You need to keep all records, invoices, receipts and statements for at least six years.

All about income tax

For most landlords, costs and income have to be accounted for in the tax year when the bill is incurred or arose rather than when it's paid or received. For example, suppose you've got a bill for repairing some windows. If the work is done in February 2012, you can deduct costs for the tax year ending 5 April 2012, even if you don't actually get the invoice until May 2012. So, if you made a big profit from renting, but have big repairs, it's worth getting them done before the end of the tax year.

Where costs and income are ongoing and spread over different tax years, like rent or insurance, then they should be split over the different tax years. So, if your rent runs from the 25th to the 24th of each month and the old tax year ends on 5 April, only twelve days of the rent would go into the old tax year, the rest should be accounted for in the new tax year.

If your annual total rent is under £15,000, the Revenue may allow income and expenditure to be recognised when it is received or paid rather than when incurred, so there will be no need to split it in this way.

What costs can be deducted from rental income?
Costs that can be deducted are the following:

- Financing costs.
- Repairs and maintenance (but not property improvements).
- Heating and lighting (where paid by the landlord).
- Insurance.
- Letting agency fees.
- Advertising for tenants.
- Accountancy fees.
- Professional and legal fees in connection with the tenancies (but not costs related to the purchase or sale of property or planning applications).
- Ground rents and service charges.
- Cleaning and gardening costs.
- Bad debts.
- Capital allowances on office or other equipment used in the course of running a property business.

- Administrative expenses including wages and also the cost of phone calls, stationery, subsistence, travel and an appropriate proportion of household expenses if you run your property business from a room in your home. (HMRC has detailed rules on what household expenses are allowed and how the proportion is calculated.)

Financing costs, including the cost of interest on any loan taken out to purchase the let property, are usually the biggest costs. If you remortgage a let property and use the funds on that property or another let property, you can deduct the interest cost of this as well. If you were to use those funds to spend on something unrelated to letting property, you may still be able to deduct the interest. The key principle is that the money must be borrowed for and used for the purposes of the property business unless you are able to show that the money you are extracting from the property business doesn't make the business balance sheet go overdrawn.

The borrowed money doesn't have to be in the form of a mortgage. Interest on a personal loan to improve a property which is then let out can be deducted too. Also, any loan or mortgage arrangement fees paid can be deducted.

Where you are paying off interest and capital on the loan, you're only allowed to deduct the interest, not the capital. Most mortgage and loan providers will, if requested, give you an annual statement showing the breakdown of interest and capital repayments.

Take care only to book costs that are wholly to do with running the lettings business and where you actually pay the costs yourself. If you're in the habit of getting tenants to pay for small repairs and then reimbursing them, you'd be on safer ground paying the supplier yourself. That way, you can more easily show that the cost is a legitimate expense.

Where a cost is split (say, half was for your own use and half for your rented property), you can apportion the cost and deduct the appropriate half as an expense.

Professional and legal fees can include membership fees of landlords' organisations, in addition to any money you pay to help with recovery of debts or any advice to do with renting such as books like this one which keep you up to date with landlord issues. However, you can't deduct legal fees or surveyors' fees on the purchase or sale of property (unless you are trading as a property developer) though you can claim them to reduce any capital gains tax liability when you later sell the property. So keep the relevant receipts safe for as long as you own the property.

When you buy furnishings for a furnished property you aren't allowed to deduct the initial cost. However, you can deduct either:

- The cost of renewals and replacements or;
- A wear and tear allowance of 10 per cent of what are called "net rents receivable" which means rents less any amounts paid by the landlord which would normally be paid by the tenant (e.g. council tax, water charges, cleaning). So if the rent is £10,000 per annum and you pay £500 council tax, the amount of wear and tear would be £950, i.e. £10,000 less £500 multiplied by 10 per cent.

Once you've elected for one or other method, that's it, you can't change each year. If renewals and replacement is claimed one year, you can't claim wear and tear allowance the next year. The method that is best for you, and which results in the biggest cost, will depend on the cost and expected life of your furnishings and the amount of the rent. Don't forget, this allowance is in addition to any costs you incur on repairs.

Bad debts can be deducted but a general provision for bad debts, e.g. 5 per cent of rents each year, isn't allowed. Administrative costs must be reasonable and capable of being supported by phone/mileage records or whatever. Again, there can't be what's called a "duality of purpose", so you can't claim for buying a newspaper because you could read the rest of the newspaper not just the property section! Also, you can't charge your time as an expense.

If it's cheaper to replace something with a more modern alternative such as replacing single glazing with equivalent double gazing the fact that this is an improvement can be disregarded and the cost *still booked as a repair* and hence deducted from rental income. The same would apply if you replaced an old kitchen with a new one with a broadly similar set and number of work tops and units of an equivalent quality.

Even where you make a loss, you must declare it, not least because you can carry it forward and set it off against rental profits in the next tax year. Indeed, UK rental losses can be carried forward as long as you have a rental business, but they disappear when your UK rental business ceases or when you die. However, you can't normally set it off against income from, say, your day job. The only exceptions to this are where the losses derive from excess capital allowances in a property business or consist of trading losses on any UK furnished holiday let (but this may change from 6 April 2011).

Property income counts as an "other" or "non-savings"

part of a taxpayer's income and is currently taxed at rates of 20 per cent, 40 per cent and 50 per cent. The same rates apply to any trading income from property development. People with income over £100,000 also lose £1 of personal allowance for every £2 by which their income is above £100,000 – which creates an "effective" income tax rate of 60 per cent on any income falling between £100,000 and £112,950. The personal allowance for the tax year ending 5 April 2011 is £6,475.

Landlords' Energy Savings Allowance (*LESA*)
This allows landlords who are paying income tax the ability to get relief at their highest marginal rate for up to £1,500 per property (£750 for two equal joint owners) for loft and cavity wall insulation, solid wall insulation, draught proofing, floor insulation and the insulation of hot water systems. This allowance is not available for furnished holiday lets.

All about capital gains tax (CGT)

Most people know that they don't have to pay capital gains tax on their main residence. However, every time you sell a property that has been rented out, you may have some capital gains tax to pay. The good news is that with a bit of planning and understanding you can significantly reduce, and often eliminate, any tax liability. So, it's worth knowing how to do it! The bad news is that CGT can be complicated (though a lot less so than it used to be) and a little boring. I'll try to keep it simple!

All about capital allowances

Certain equipment used mainly for your letting business, such as office equipment, furniture and garden tools, etc, qualifies for a capital allowance though, if there is private use, the cost must be apportioned. You cannot get allowances for furniture and fittings in residential property but you could claim allowances for the office chair you used yourself.

A writing down allowance of 20 per cent is available each year, calculated on a reducing balance basis. Alternatively you can claim a 100 per cent annual investment allowance for expenditure up to £100,000 per business. The £100,000 limit only exists for 2010/11 and 2011/12. This reduces to £25,000 for 2012/13.

The Government is currently reviewing capital allowances and changes look likely for future tax years. Check with HMRC for the latest position.

What is a capital gain and how do you calculate it? Obviously, you need to calculate the amount of capital gain. This is the "net proceeds" from selling the property less the total costs of buying it.

The first thing is to work out the net proceeds. This is simply the price the property sold for, less all the costs associated with selling it, including advertising costs, estate agents' fees and legal costs. (If you sold the property to a relative other than your spouse or to anyone else at below market value, the Revenue will insist that the figure used is the market value of the property.)

The second thing is to work out the cost of the property. This is the basic cost when it was bought plus all the costs associated with buying it (this would include stamp duty land tax, legal fees, surveys you initiated, etc) plus the cost of any enhancements made during the time it was owned (building a conservatory, adding a loft or costs of making it habitable and fit for letting). If you inherited the property from a relation or friend the basic cost is the market value used for probate purposes at the time you acquired it.

You then simply deduct the total buying costs from the net proceeds at sale and you have the capital gain. So, if your costs of buying the property plus enhancements were £100,000 and your net proceeds after selling costs were £220,000, the gain is £120,000.

Principal private residence (PPR) and private letting relief (PLR) exemptions
If you ever lived in the property you get a whole raft of exemptions. Every unmarried person and each married couple is entitled to what is known as "Principal Private Residence" (PPR) relief on their only or main residence. What's less well-known is that this exemption can be extended to cover any period where the let property was your main residence *plus in each property, your last three years of ownership.*

Tip 1

If you've bought a property that requires substantial construction work before it can be occupied as your main residence, the PPR exemption can be extended for up to a year. You can also extend it if you're unable to occupy it due to a delay in selling your old property. In this situation, it's possible to have both properties covered by the PPR exemption.

Tip 2

If you have more than one main residence you should tell the Revenue which is your main one within two years of acquiring the second. Obviously, this must be your own private residence where you habitually live, not a property that you rent out. If you are lucky enough to have two homes that you can live in (neither of which is rented) and fail to nominate one, the Revenue may make a nomination for you based on the facts. If you live in both, choose the one that will have the biggest capital gain or perhaps the one you wish to sell first as your PPR. Once you have elected a property as a PPR, you can change it at any time by writing to the Revenue. However, it will only be effective for a period beginning less than two years before the date of your election to change.

Tip 3

If you take in a lodger in your own home, your PPR exemption will usually not be affected but if any part of your property is used *exclusively* for business purposes, the PPR exemption is not available for that part of the property for the period in question. However, if you have an office at home and only sometimes use it for other home uses, then the PPR exemption is still usable in full.

So, suppose you bought a property in year 0 and sold it in year 7 and you lived in it from year 0 to year 4 as your main residence but rented it out thereafter. The first four years wouldn't count as it was your main residence but the last three years wouldn't count either – i.e. there would be no CGT to pay.

Now, suppose you rented out the property for longer – say, up to year ten. In this case, there may still be no CGT to pay. The reason is that another very useful and significant relief called "Private Letting Relief" (PLR), comes into play! This Private Letting relief is the lowest of:

1. The amount of gain already exempted under PPR.
2. The gain as a consequence of the letting period.
3. £40,000.

Private Letting Relief applies to any property which qualifies for exemption under PPR and which has been let *at any time* during the ownership of the taxpayer. In our example we already know that the first four years that you lived in the property as your main residence are exempt plus another three years out of the ten – i.e. 7/10 (seven out of ten) years of the gain is exempt. This leaves only 3/10 (three out of the ten) years chargeable.

If the gain was £90,000, the amount that is chargeable would be 3/10 x £90,000 = £27,000.

The amount exempted under PPR would be 7/10 x £90,000 = £63,000.

As the lowest figure of £27,000, £63,000 and £40,000, is £27,000, this amount is also automatically exempted as a result of PLR.

The chargeable gain before PLR of £27,000 (i.e. 3/10 x £90,000) less PLR of £27,000 leaves zero gain! As you can see, the Revenue is exceedingly generous to landlords who let out their former homes.

It's also good to know that the £40,000 Private Letting Relief applies to every property which has even been your only or main residence at any time during your ownership – so even if you sell two previous homes during one tax year, you could still get up to £40,000 of PLR on each property! And joint owners each get £40,000 of PLR.

Those familiar with UK politics will know that some of our MPs were effectively "flipping" between properties on a grand scale. Following the outcry over this, it is thought by some that some of the PLR exemptions and the PPR extension of three years could be cut in a future budget.

However, for now, the combination of PPR and PLR still remains a very powerful way to cut tax bills for people with a former home they now wish to dispose of and for anyone planning a future of tax-free capital growth.

Because PPR works by giving you exemption for the period you lived in the property *plus, in each property, your last three years of ownership,* this exemption works best if you move into the property as your main residence straight after purchase.

To be a main residence and to get PPR, you must *genuinely* live in the property and in borderline cases HMRC will look at the address on your tax return and where your utility bills and bank statements go among a number of other factors to establish the "true quality" of your occupation.

Annual exemption

Each taxpayer gets an annual exemption from CGT. In the year 2010–2011 it's £10,100 and the amount usually goes up each year. So, if you had a potential capital gain of £13,000, and your exemption is £10,100, you'll have to pay tax on £2,900.

Tip 4

If you own a property with your spouse, any income or capital gain will be split between both of you in whatever proportion you own it and each person can apply his own CGT annual exemption to his part of the gain. Where husband and wife pay tax at different rates, it's worth planning to share ownership of the property in a way that minimises total tax liability. For jointly held properties, each person will also have a £40,000 limit for Private Letting Relief. Even if you already own it, it's possible to follow a simple legal process to have it transferred into joint or multi ownership but it's best to do this before the property is put on the market for sale. There are no CGT consequences in transferring ownership between husband and wife though there could be stamp duty land tax to pay if the property is mortgaged. There may be CGT consequences if you transfer ownership to other family members or non-relatives.

Tip 5

If you buy a new residence whilst keeping the old one for letting, you could nominate the new one as the PPR within two years of buying it, but gain the PPR exemption on the old one too for the last three years before you sell it (provided that you had lived in it). In this way you can gain exemptions on two residences at once for up to three years. However, if you nominate a property as your PPR, you *must* have genuinely lived there for at least part of the time.

Tip 6

As part of the PPR exemption, the Revenue provides concessions when you can't live in your house because of work requirements and if your job takes you overseas.

You can offset any capital losses, including losses from previous years, against any chargeable gains. So, if you make a good gain on a property but lost a load on shares you sold, then you can offset the losses of one against the other.

With a bit of luck, and if you've used all the relief and exemptions available to you, you may have found you have no capital gains tax liability at all! Give yourself a pat on the back! If you do have some, you'll need to work out how much tax you actually have to pay. This is easy.

For capital gains arising after 23 June 2010, CGT is payable at either 18 per cent by basic rate taxpayers or 28 per cent by higher rate taxpayers, though an entrepreneurs' rate of 10 per cent may be available for landlords with furnished holiday letting properties.

The higher rate of 28 per cent applies to capital gains made by people between 23 June 2010 and 5 April 2011 whose taxable income for the year ending 5 April 2011 (after deducting their personal allowance and any other available deductions) plus their capital gains between 23 June 2010 and 5 April 2011 was above the income tax basic rate band for that year which was £37,400.

Basic rate taxpayers will pay CGT at 18 per cent on the first part of any gains which arose between 23 June 2010 and 5 April 2011 until their basic rate band is exhausted. After that point they will be taxed at 28 per cent.

If you happen to have a capital gain arising between 6 April 2008 and 22 June 2010 the rate of CGT was a single flat rate of just 18 per cent and gains arising between 6 April 2010 and 22 June 2010 will not count in working out how much of an individual's basic rate band for the tax year ending April 5 2011 has been used.

For the tax year ending 5 April 2012 it looks like the two main rates of CGT of 18 per cent and 28 per cent will continue to apply, though the 2011 budget may amend this.

The total amount of CGT must be paid by 31 January following the end of the tax year in question.

Tax on UK and European Economic Area (EEA) holiday lets

To qualify as a "holiday" let, the property must be furnished to a degree necessary for normal occupation, available to let to the public for at least 140 days a year and actually be let for at least seventy days a year. Lettings must be at market rents, not peppercorn rents to friends as the letting must be commercial, i.e. with a view to making profits.

With a furnished holiday let you can also claim rollover relief on replacement of business assets, capital allowances on the costs of fixtures and fittings (though the wear and tear allowance is not available), and you can "roll over" all capital gains onto another UK holiday let property, provided that the full amount of the sale proceeds is rolled over within one year before or three years after the initial sale. UK holiday lets require separate accounts to be kept. Losses may be set off against other income from the same tax year or the previous one. The lower entrepreneurs' rate should also be available for these lets if the whole business is sold.

The taxation of furnished holiday lets is being reviewed by the current government and a new regime will apply from 6 April 2011 which is likely to include an increase in the number of days a property must be available for letting, the number of days it's actually let for and probably also changes to the rules on loss relief.

Tip 7
CGT liability can be deferred or your income tax liability reduced if you reinvest your profit in a Venture Capital Trust or Enterprise Investment Scheme. However, be wary as VCTs and EISs are at the risky end of company investment and you could lose the lot! Check the trust or scheme out carefully. Only an investment in an EIS will defer CGT.

Tip 8

Be honest with the Revenue. Fraud is illegal and there are high penalties. The Revenue has a powerful database of who owns what and they do a large number of investigations each year. Some will be random and some will be triggered by information they hold directly, obtained from other sources or from information that you yourself have given.

Tip 9

Keep all your receipts, bank records, statements as well as contracts for sale and purchase for at least six years and for as long as you own the property if they count as a deductible cost against capital gains. You'll need these if you are subject to a Revenue investigation.

Tax on other foreign holiday lets

Where a property is let abroad, none of the additional relief allowed on UK or EEA holiday lets is allowed. However, travelling expenses are allowed if incurred wholly for the purposes of the overseas let. Some UK investors have bought abroad using offshore companies to avoid local land taxes but this may have complex implications. If you are thinking of doing this, it's worth discussing your plans with an accountant who is an expert in this area.

The rent a room scheme

If you rent out a room in your home, you won't have to pay any income tax if the rent is below a certain amount. At present this is £4,250 per annum.

Canny investors know that if they buy a property for their son to live in whilst at university and the property is put in his name, he can then rent out a room and get the rent a room relief as well as benefit from his own personal income tax and capital gains tax allowance. Of course, the property must be his and not all parents feel happy with being quite so generous.

All about stamp duty land tax

Stamp duty on home purchases applies as follows: 0 per cent up to £125,000, 1 per cent up to £250,000, 3 per cent up to £500,000 and 4 per cent over that figure. It's important to appreciate that this tax applies to the whole of the purchase price so a small change in purchase price can make a huge difference to the tax payable.

Expect this tax to go up further in the future too and look out, in particular, for a hike for properties over £1m to 5 per cent. One little ray of sunshine is that in some disadvantaged areas, provided that the purchase price is under £150,000, no stamp duty land tax is payable. The HMRC site lists these areas. Under a temporary measure, first-time buyers who have never bought before are currently exempt from stamp duty land tax up to £250,000. If there are two or more purchasers both must never have bought before.

Tip 10

If you move abroad and become non-resident in the UK and non UK ordinarily resident, and then sell your investment properties, all the gain should be CGT free if you remain non-resident for five full tax years. If you've been letting your own home while working temporarily abroad, your PPR relief is still available for the time you are away.

Tip 11

If you are purely buying and developing property as a business no CGT applies at all, but there will be income tax to pay on any profits you make in selling your property.

Tip 12

Moveable fittings escape stamp duty land tax but HMRC will carefully scrutinise transactions where the cost of moveable fittings bought with the property appears excessive.

Tip 13

It can be a really smart move from a tax point of view to let out your existing home to fund the purchase of a new property for you to live in because (1) both properties will attract PPR (because of the three year rule) thus meriting a saving on potential capital gains and (2) equity in the former home can be released via a mortgage loan and used for any purpose whilst the interest on the loan (up to the value of the property when first rented out) can be deducted from rental income thus saving income tax. You may even be able to avoid the need to take out any mortgage at all on your new home.

Tip 14

An allowance called the "Flat Conversion Allowance" is useful if you are thinking of converting vacant flats above commercial property back into residential use though there are a number of qualifying criteria you need to meet.

Tip 15

If you expect to be in a higher tax bracket next tax year and there is a profit on your property letting business, consider delaying maintenance expenditure until the next tax year if it helps reduce income tax liability. Conversely, reduce CGT liability by selling in a tax year when taxable income will put you in the lower CGT band.

Tip 16

Keep your tax liability under regular review and remember that just because most loans used for the purposes of letting property are tax deductible, this is not a good reason to over borrow and risk bankruptcy. Also, don't remortgage constantly and end up giving yourself a huge future capital gains tax liability that you cannot afford to pay.

Tip 17

Landlords who are only letting property should not register as self employed. Self employment attracts National Insurance but rental income doesn't.

> *Tip 18*
> This chapter is only a rough guide to a very complex
> subject. HMRC publishes detailed guidance and notes
> on what is allowed and what isn't but there are still grey
> areas. Check their guides and if in doubt seek the advice
> of an experienced advisor in this area.

Investing via a property company

Some people set up a limited company to run their rental
business. The main attraction is that corporation tax is
lower than the higher rate of income tax and companies
also continue to be eligible for indexation relief on their
capital gains. But, people thinking of doing this should
bear in mind that a company doesn't get PPR or PLR
relief or an annual exemption from capital gains. Also,
there may be tax to pay when taking profits out of the
company and you'll have the cost of setting up the
company and making annual returns each year too.

Whether it's worth setting up a property company will
depend on your own circumstances. The advice of an
accountant with a good understanding of investment
property and company and personal taxation is recommended.

The death of "SIPPS" and the birth of "REITS"

In 2005 the Chancellor, Gordon Brown, came up with an
incredible idea. His idea was to allow people to put
residential property, including property which was let out
(and holiday lets) as well as many other types of investments, into what are called Self-invested Personal Pension
Schemes (SIPPS).

SIPPS are an existing type of pension fund in which you have more control of the investments (though they are administered by a scheme administrator). They have been around since 1989 but previously you could only put commercial properties into one.

Mr Brown's idea meant that if you wanted to contribute to your pension scheme to buy specific properties, you would get tax relief on the money you put in. So, if you wanted to purchase a £100,000 property, you'd only need to put in £78,000 if you were a basic rate taxpayer. If you were a higher rate taxpayer, it was going to be even better in that you'd effectively only need to contribute £60,000.

Once the property was in the SIPP fund, the rent would have been re-invested in the fund and used to pay off the mortgage, but it would (subject to certain conditions) be free from income tax and from capital gains tax when you sold it.

You could even borrow up to 50 per cent of the total value of the pension fund.

So if you wanted to buy a £150,000 property with your pension, you could make a contribution of £60,000, which would be boosted to £100,000 if you were a higher rate taxpayer by the tax relief, plus the fund could then borrow the remaining 50 per cent.

There were a few drawbacks in the small print, but basically the whole thing was pretty attractive as a tax avoidance wheeze and, as usual with such wheezes, the people who were thought most likely to benefit were wealthy people, especially those who got big bonuses and who could put most of their earnings for a year into a SIPP, thus avoiding income tax altogether.

Well, fairly predictably I think, the whole financial

services industry went wild and thousands of hours were spent designing and marketing schemes, and the nation's financial advisers worked long into the nights.

Gradually though, concerns began to emerge. First, given the existing high prices of property and the fact that many people were struggling to get on the housing ladder, wouldn't all the new money from investors drive prices further up and out of the reach of the first-time buyer?

Second, as the people who would benefit most would be those on high earnings who could afford to put the maximum in, wasn't the concept inequitable?

Third, since sales of SIPPS would not initially be regulated, there was a real risk of mis-selling.

Fourth, and this was probably the clincher for the Chancellor, wouldn't it all lead to a big loss in potential tax revenues?

Well, in December 2005, the Chancellor did a massive U turn and effectively shelved the whole idea of putting individual properties in a SIPP.

There does, however, remain one other rather neat way that SIPPS can still be made to work.

If you put your money in a "syndicate" you can still qualify for tax breaks within the pension fund rules. The syndicate must contain at least three properties, be worth at least one million pounds and owned by at least eleven investors (because you are not allowed to have over 10 per cent of the holding). This spreads the risk over a number of properties. All eleven investors must be "unconnected" and you have to think carefully about what happens when any individual wants to sell.

Where hotel rooms or other holiday accommodation is bought by the syndicate, any personal use of the property by a member of the scheme is not allowed. Annual management fees are not cheap.

In 2007 the Chancellor gave the go-ahead to another new type of property investment vehicle with no tax charge, called Real Estate Investment Trusts (REITS) to produce a more "liquid market" with investors able to buy and sell shares in the REITS rather than buying or selling properties themselves.

However, investors are taxed on the income they receive from the REIT and on gains made when selling their investment in the REIT though income tax can be reclaimed if they invest via a pension or an ISA. Income and gains distributed are treated as property income although, unfortunately, you cannot set your other property losses against this income.

12

JET TO LET: DIVERSIFYING YOUR PROPERTY PORTFOLIO

There are many ways to diversify in property. Many people start off with a basic longer-term let property. However, there are of course other opportunities; in holiday lets both in the UK and abroad as well as in lets to longer term tenants in overseas markets. As the world has become smaller and more integrated, buying overseas where property is cheaper is becoming increasingly attractive to UK investors, a phenomenon which is now wittily called "jet to let".

By investing in different types of letting market you can spread your risk too. However, these alternatives usually involve more work and higher costs. This chapter looks at these alternatives in detail.

UK and EEA holiday lets

Buying a holiday let has become increasingly attractive in recent years. The capital gains tax treatment for UK holiday lets (see Chapter 11, page 239) has generally been kinder than for standard buy-to-lets though this is now under review. You don't usually need to worry about people not leaving when they should and you don't need a formal tenancy agreement either (though it's sensible to keep documentation to prove that it was your intention that the let was just for a holiday).

Also attractive is the fact that property prices in UK coastal resorts have tended to do very well in recent years, helped in part by people buying second homes for their own use as well as for holiday lets and by generally warmer weather. I expect these trends to continue.

However, running costs are higher than in longer-term lets. You'll have more periods when the property is empty but you will still have to pay insurance (which will be higher because the property is empty), utilities and council tax. You'll also need to have good security in place to deter would-be squatters and burglars and there will be marketing costs and the cost of cleaning between lets to consider too. Finally, you will need a local person who can be relied upon to maintain things promptly and deal with emergencies.

Getting finance may be harder too. Few lenders offer mortgages on holiday lets because of the higher risk of default so you may have to fall back on a commercial loan or approach a mortgage broker. The deposit may be higher too.

However, if you can get it right you can do very well on holiday lets. The key is to buy in an area where you can let it out for most of the year, preferably for periods of a few weeks at a time. As with any other letting pro-position, look for areas where demand is high and supply of other properties is low and where changes are coming to make the area more attractive. For example, if a new leisure complex is planned or the roads are being improved this should bring more holidaymakers into the area, so demand can be expected to rise.

Investing in property abroad

In the last few years there has been a massive increase in interest in buying property abroad. Right now it seems you can hardly turn on your television without another programme showing happy people jumping on planes to buy overseas. The trend is driven in part by rising British property prices. Property abroad is usually cheaper, often considerably so. The opening up of new destinations by budget airlines and cheaper air fares has also helped things along.

Buying abroad can work really well but there are things you need to be aware of. For a start, the legal systems in other countries will be very different. In most places you will be committed at an earlier stage than would be the case at home. It can be difficult just establishing a good legal title to the property and even confirming that the person you are buying from really does own it in the first place! Checking rights of way over land can be more complex and there may be differences in the way that planning permission operates too.

Of course, properties can run the full gamut from ready to move into up to major restoration projects. If you are doing up a property, it will be more difficult if language is a barrier and if you are not on site to control things. In some areas, properties must be renovated or built using local materials and techniques, thereby raising costs. Even with brand-new properties there may be unusual residents' regulations to comply with. Also, property taxes, legal fees, land registry and mortgage costs all tend to be higher outside the UK.

The advice contained in all the earlier chapters of this book applies equally well to buying abroad. Just as in the UK, you need to do your own research and keep an open but slightly sceptical mind. Read all you can about an area and speak to as many people as possible, especially people who can be relied upon to give you impartial advice.

Even more than in the UK you need to employ good lawyers, architects, surveyors and builders, so you must spend some time checking their credentials to ensure you've got the best people working with you. Also, talk to people who have done it before and find out what problems they found and how they overcame them.

There are many reasons for buying abroad. You can buy to live in it permanently as your main home, as a holiday home for your own occasional use or with the intention to let it out either as holiday accommodation or for longer-term lettings. In fact, people often buy for a mix of all these reasons. For example, someone may buy a second home that they will ultimately retire to but will in the meantime use as a means of generating income from holiday or longer-term lets as well as for the odd holiday for themselves.

It's OK to have a mix of reasons for buying, but, if you do, it's important to set out what your objectives are, how much you wish to spend, how much you think the property will bring in rent (if that's your intention) and what the costs will be. If you are thinking of ultimately retiring there at a later date, think about how suitable the property will be when you're that much older. Also, check with the Department for Work and Pensions if you will be able to access your British pension overseas. The state of local healthcare and whether you qualify for free or reduced cost care is also worth looking into. The

Department of Health can advise on what you are entitled to.

Of course, if you are buying purely as an investment then your own personal preferences won't count at all. In many ways this is easier than trying to balance investment with buying for your own use because you can focus on things like demand, occupancy, advertising, agent fees and rent, unencumbered by any other personal objectives.

Holiday homes

A good holiday home must be easily marketable and accessible to prospective holidaymakers. Outside the main tourist areas there may be a more authentic feel, but if it's too far from the nearest airport, up a long bumpy road and miles from the nearest shop, people will be put off. The main seaside tourist areas will invariably be more expensive and will get good rents but may be difficult to let outside the summer season. Properties in major cities may be attractive for year-round holiday lettings and for the longer-term tenant market. It all depends on local demand and supply so you need to do your research on each specific location following the guidelines set out in Chapter 3.

If your property is served by a single local airport and a single budget airline there is a risk that they could stop flying to that destination. If your lettings market is wider and people can reach your accommodation by other means your risk will be less.

Someone reliable must be on hand to deal with changeovers, cleaning, maintenance and any on the spot problems.

Don't forget to check out local holiday letting rules and regulations and do occasional checks to ensure the local agency is not letting out and failing to pass on the money.

Co-Ownership, Time-Shares and Leaseback

There are many variations on holiday-home ownership. You could buy with other owners so that each of you has a share of the property or you could sell time-shares to others on a commercial basis. This would, of course, involve a special form of legal contract and consideration of what would happen if someone wanted to pull out or sell his share. Another alternative, popular in France, is the "leaseback" scheme in which you buy the property then lease it back to a developer or manager who guarantees a fixed income and/or an agreed number of weeks for your own use. Again, have the small print carefully checked.

Longer-term tenants

In the longer-term tenant market you'll need to check out the local tenancy laws and regulations carefully. These will differ hugely from the UK and you need to find out the procedure in whatever country you invest in. If you are a member of a UK landlord association it might be able to put you in touch with other landlords who run long-term lets abroad.

You may find that longer-term tenants will have more protection than they do at home so it may well prove much harder to evict a bad tenant. Also, rent controls may exist which may set a limit on what you can charge. In Central and Eastern Europe, with the exception of top notch properties, rents tend to be a lot less than in the UK, because salaries are still so much lower than here in the UK.

Things you need to know

Whether investing for the holiday market or for longer-term tenants the logistics of the arrangement will be more difficult if you are not based locally. You therefore need to budget for the costs of marketing the property, maintaining and insuring it, paying agency and service charges, cleaning it and dealing with any local issues as they come up. It's worth checking even before you buy that you'll be allowed to let it out in the first place, what safety measures you have to comply with and how to account for your income locally.

For property buying, selling and renting you need a good local lawyer. You can find lists of British solicitors with offices outside the UK from the Law Society. Also, the Foreign Office has lists of English-speaking lawyers abroad. In many European countries you'll also have to deal with a public notary. In Europe, the notary is usually a civil servant (not a lawyer) whose job it is to check the title deeds, draw up contracts and make a record of the sale. However, it is not part of a notary's job to advise you, so you'll still need to appoint a lawyer. For lawyers and notaries, make sure you take time to check their credentials with their local body.

Although you'll probably want to employ a local architect and surveyor, the Royal Institute of British Architects and the Royal Institution of Chartered Surveyors are worth talking to first. Both have databases of practitioners abroad. If you can, get a local person so as not to offend local sensibilities.

Getting finance

More UK banks are lending on foreign properties, sometimes in foreign currency, and banks in Central and

Eastern Europe too are increasingly waking up to buy-to-let. Also, mortgage brokers can usually be relied upon to source finance. Borrowing locally from a foreign bank may involve paying higher fees and the lenders in more remote markets may only look at your net income to assess whether you can afford it rather than taking any note of rent to income multiples.

Fixing the exchange rate
When you buy abroad you'll always be at the mercy of exchange rates (although if Britain joins the Euro, this will cease to be a problem in most of Europe). If you are buying a property off-plan or which must be paid for in stages, you could fix the rate by buying the currency now. If you don't have the money, you could buy a forward contract with a bank. Of course, the whole time you own the property, exchange rates could go either way which will affect the value of your investment!

Getting insurance

Most British insurance brokers offer good insurance policies from well-known insurers for places like Spain, Portugal and France. This avoids the complications of a policy written in a foreign language. Check that you are covered for the period between exchange and completion, for unoccupied periods and for the cost of emergency travel and temporary accommodation following a big claim.

Unfortunately, for many countries, cover for a foreign property is only considered if your UK home is insured with the same insurance company. For more out of the way countries, you may have to seek out an insurer in the country concerned. Policies may be quite different though. For example, subsidence and flooding cover is not covered at all in some countries and public liability cover may not extend to holidaymakers or tenants!

Watch out for "community insurance" and residents' schemes too, as these are often limited in what they cover. Finally, if you end up in dispute with a local insurer you'll have the expense and hassle of having to fight it out in a foreign court.

Investigate the risk of hurricanes, tornadoes, earthquakes, floods, landslides and even tsunamis in the locality and try to get cover for these risks. Local insurers may be more prepared than UK ones to consider these risks as they'll have more data. If the property is out of action for a long time following, say, a hurricane it will not be generating revenue either. Can you finance this yourself or can you insure against this risk? If the property is unoccupied for a long time, you may be able to reduce the premium by paying someone locally to look after it on a regular basis.

Where to buy and what to buy abroad

The most popular countries for Brits to invest in have long been Spain, France and Portugal. These countries are also close to the UK and relatively easy to get to. Prices have been moving down for a few years in most areas and some observers think the massive oversupply of new building in some parts will continue to drive down rents and house prices in the medium term.

But even these established markets are not without other risks. For example, in recent years many British buyers were running scared of Valencia's so called "land grab" law in which local developers could compulsorily purchase land from existing owners because cowboy developers had reclassified land without first asking the land owner's permission.

Other places that seem to be attracting the interest of British investors are Eastern Europe and Cyprus as well as more far-flung places like the USA, South Africa and Dubai. In the case of the Czech Republic, and all the other new EU countries, membership of the EU and the additional stability that brings drove prices up sharply for a time though they have stabilised. Whether they can produce a decent return to investors will depend, as ever, upon the type of property, the area it's in, the market for tenants and/or tourists, exchange rates and whether the local market becomes oversupplied. The Bulgarian coast has suffered from oversupply leading to falling prices and diminished rents in recent years.

Other countries that are attracting speculative investments are Croatia, Turkey, Northern Cyprus, Morocco, Brazil and Cape Verde. All these new markets are at risk from over supply because the temptation for local governments and land owners to sell huge tracts of land to build holiday homes to wealthy people from Western Europe and North America is very great indeed.

If you read the previous chapters, you'll know there are good places and less good places to buy within any country or city. Do your research and look out for areas that are changing for the better. For example, Benidorm recently spent lots of money to shed its old image and set up stylish theme parks and golf courses. Look out for regeneration initiatives and change that will drive an area forward.

Check what will happen near to your preferred location. If you bought for that sea view, check that the land in front of you can't be built on and find out about planning restrictions generally. Some councils have tight planning laws meaning that the area will not be swamped with hundreds of me-too or high-rise developments while others have an anything goes approach.

If a big new airport or connecting road is being built, that's good news if you are in the holiday letting business, provided that you aren't under the flight path or too close to the motorway!

All about taxes on foreign property

Wherever you invest there is one constant: tax! As long as you are a UK resident, you are liable to UK income taxes on rental profits from properties abroad as well as capital gains tax on the money you make when you sell. The only exceptions are for people who come from another country (called "non-domiciled").

It's beyond the scope of this book to look at domicile as it's quite a complex area (more permanent than residence but different from nationality!). However, it's worth saying that a non-domiciled taxpayer is only taxable on profits or capital gains from foreign investments if and when they bring money back to the UK. This means that if you are a married couple where one of you is non-domiciled, you could make foreign investments in the name of the non-domiciled person and free from UK tax as long as no funds are remitted to the UK.

Starting in the tax year 2008–9 "non-doms" have to pay tax on all income and gains wherever they arose or instead pay a £30,000 charge. Check with a tax expert first for the latest position.

If you are UK-domiciled but have emigrated you'll be exempt from UK tax on foreign property (though you will still be taxed on income from any UK property you own). So if you want to invest abroad for the long term and also emigrate at some point, you may be better off investing overseas. Once you have emigrated you will be exempt from UK capital gains tax whether the properties are in the UK or abroad. However, you must stay away for at least five whole UK tax years or else the Revenue can claw back capital gains tax.

Many people set up companies as a vehicle to invest in property abroad especially if they are going to invest for the long term. In some countries too, investing through a local company may be the only way that you, as a foreigner, can actually buy property. If you don't intend to emigrate, it may be a good thing to use a UK company as a vehicle to invest, but it will depend on your own circumstances and how long you want to invest for, so speak to tax advisers in both countries.

If you intend to emigrate (or you are non-UK domiciled) you'll want to avoid using a UK company for foreign investments. Indeed many British investors have bought abroad using companies which are based offshore to avoid local land taxes. However, this may have complex implications. If you are thinking of doing this, it's worth discussing your plans with an accountant who is an expert in this area. If you do set up an offshore company it must be set up and run properly. It's not cheap either, and income and gains while the controlling shareholder is still a UK resident will be taxable in the UK.

As well as UK taxes you'll also need to consider local taxes which are often higher than in the UK. Many countries will tax foreign property owners on their income and capital gains. Our Government does allow some relief through something called "double tax relief" which is intended to ensure you are not taxed twice, but you are still taxed at the higher of the two countries' rates of tax!

So, if the foreign tax exceeds your UK liability, your double tax relief is limited to the amount of your UK tax bill, thus reducing it to nil. In other words, our Government won't compensate you for the higher tax burdens you face in a foreign land!

When investing abroad think beyond income, capital gains and stamp duty land tax types of taxes. Other countries often have many other weird and strange forms of tax that we don't have. Double tax relief will not apply for these taxes because there is no UK equivalent and even foreign land taxes, the equivalent of stamp duty land tax, cannot be set off against any UK tax. So, find out about every other type of tax or fee that can be applied to your type of investment *before* you invest.

Finally, it's worth noting that schemes to avoid tax could be based on loopholes that are already closed by the local government or are about to be. If you cheat the local government of their tax, you could face consequences. For example, in some countries, it's common for people to pay local land taxes on the basis of the price declared in the deed of sale and not what was actually paid. If you are found out there could be heavy penalties including compulsory state purchase of the property plus big fines. As in life, there's really no such thing as a free lunch!

Other opportunities

If you are an active investor, lots of other opportunities may come your way. Some of these may give you an element of diversification. For example, people may ask you to look after their properties for them – in effect, acting as a managing letting agent. Other people may come to you with schemes to invest in. Two new ones doing the rounds in the last few years have been units in large managed student halls of residence and single apartments in hotels – the latter having the attraction of potentially being "SIPPable".

Look at every opportunity as just that, an opportunity! Appraise each one dispassionately and plan for the future. Good luck and successful investing!

Appendix 1

A SAMPLE ASSURED SHORTHOLD TENANCY AGREEMENT

Where necessary, and by way of explanation, I have included in *italics* in square brackets my own comments.

Assured Shorthold Tenancy Agreement

This agreement is made **INSERT DATE** between **INSERT LANDLORD'S NAME**, who is referred to here as "the landlord", and **INSERT TENANT'S NAME(S)**, who is referred to here as "the tenant", who, if more than one, are each jointly, individually and severally liable under this agreement.

("Jointly and severally" means that if the tenant shares the cost of the tenancy with another tenant, then if one does not pay his share, the landlord will seek the balance of the rent owing in full from either tenant.)

By this agreement the landlord lets and the tenant takes all of those rooms of the property known as **INSERT NAME AND FULL ADDRESS OF PROPERTY** hereafter referred to as "the property" together with the fixtures, fittings, furniture and effects therein (as set out in the Inventory) for a term of six months, starting at **INSERT START DATE** and ending at Noon on **INSERT END DATE**.

The tenant agrees that if the property is permanently vacated by the tenant at the tenant's own request before the last day of the term, the tenant shall remain liable to pay to the landlord the full unpaid balance of the rent receivable by the landlord had this agreement run the full term.

If the tenant is unable to pay rent until the end of the fixed term but finds another tenant prepared to take on the property, then, provided that the new tenant is acceptable to the landlord, the landlord will be prepared to accept the tenant's request to close the tenancy early, though the tenant will be liable for the landlord's reasonable costs associated with the re-letting.

The rent amount is **INSERT AMOUNT** pounds per calendar month payable in advance. The tenant agrees to pay the rent in advance by a single bank standing order by the **INSERT DATE OF RENT PAYMENT** day of each month without deduction or set off. *[The rent money should leave the tenant's account six days before the due date, as this will allow time for inter-bank transfers and long weekends. If more than one tenant, get them to set up just one standing order.]*

The payment of the first month's rent is due on signature of this agreement. If any rent or other money payable by the tenant is not paid within seven days of the day on which it is due, it shall be payable with interest at the rate of 4 per cent per annum above the base minimum lending rate of **INSERT ANY UK BANK**

NAME. This will be calculated on a day to day basis, from the day upon which it became due. If payment of rent is not received on the date it is due and the landlord needs to write to or visit the tenant, an additional administration fee may be charged to the tenant.

The tenant also agrees to pay the landlord on the signature of this agreement a deposit of **INSERT AMOUNT OF DEPOSIT** as security against the failure by the tenant to make good any demand by the landlord, and at the tenant's expense any damage by the tenant to the property or to any fixtures and fittings, furnishing and effects and as security against any expense or other nuisance caused to the landlord by the failure of the tenant to behave in a tenant-like manner or to return the property to the condition in which it was let (fair wear and tear excepted).

This deposit will be held by the landlord as stakeholder and lodged with a tenancy deposit protection scheme through the term of the tenancy without any deduction being made. The tenant will be advised by the landlord within 14 days of the start of the tenancy which scheme is protecting the deposit. No interest will be paid on the deposit.

[For all new assured shorthold tenancies in England and Wales from 6 April 2007, where you take a deposit (see Chapter 8), you will have to give to the tenant, within fourteen days, details of the tenancy deposit scheme you are in. You could include these details on the tenancy agreement. Scotland is likely to bring in a similar scheme soon.]

If, at the end of the six-month term, the tenant wants to continue the tenancy and has not received from the landlord two months' notice to end the tenancy, it will carry on from month to month as a monthly periodic tenancy. The arrangements in section 21 of the Housing Act 1988 for the landlord to repossess the property apply to this agreement. This means the tenant cannot claim any legal rights to stay on once the tenancy has ended and a court order says the tenant must leave.

The landlord may seek to start action to repossess the property if the tenant fails to pay rent fourteen days after it is due, if the tenant becomes bankrupt, if any of the grounds listed in Schedule 2 of the Housing Act 1988 as amended by the Housing Act 1996 apply (these include not paying the rent, breaking the tenancy terms and causing a nuisance or annoyance) or if the arrangements for the landlord to repossess in section 21 of the Housing Act 1988 apply. The landlord will obtain a court order to repossess.

Should the property be the landlord's main or principal home before the start of the tenancy agreement, the provisions for recovery of possession by the landlord in schedule 2 of the Housing Act 1988 will apply.

[If applicable you should also include this clause: The property is subject to a mortgage granted before the start date of this tenancy agreement which gives the mortgagee the power of sale and that possession of the property may be recovered by the mortgagee under the provisions of Schedule 2 Ground 2 of the Housing Act 1988.]

Deposit

Provided that the tenant has vacated the property and has returned all keys to the property to the landlord, the deposit shall be returned to the tenant following the end of the tenancy. It will be returned after deducting any rent and other sums referred to that may be owed by the tenant – the reasons for these deductions will be notified to the tenant in writing.

The contents of the property shall be assumed to be in good order unless noted otherwise on the inventory.

Occupation only by the tenant
The tenant agrees not to sub-let or part with all or a share of possession or occupation of the property without the consent of the landlord (whose consent shall not unreasonably be withheld).

Utilities
In addition to the rent, the tenant is responsible for payment of all utilities including council tax, water rates and/or charges, electricity, gas, telephone and TV licence during the term of the tenancy, for making arrangements for meter readings at the start and end of the tenancy and advising the landlord of the readings. *[You need to check meter readings too but having the tenant do it will save some time on move-in/out days!]*

General
The tenant **must not**:

1. Make any alteration or addition to the property.
2. Damage the property or the fixtures, fittings or furnishings or remove them from the property. No screws, nails or bolts are to be attached to any wall or part of the property and no "blu-tack" or similar

substance may be attached to walls. *[Put in a few picture hooks and tell the tenant he must only hang pictures on these.]*

3. Dismantle any item of furniture. *[Some tenants may dismantle and store your furniture if they plan to put in their own. If you've ever tried putting self-assembled furniture together after it's been disassembled, you'll know why this clause is here!]*

4. Bring in any item of furniture that doesn't comply with the Furnishings Fire Safety Regulations.

5. Interfere with the internal or external decorations of the property.

6. Change or alter any locks on any door or window. (If any keys have been lost, the tenant must notify the landlord and pay the landlord the cost of fitting new locks and obtaining replacement keys.)

7. Have any additional keys made without permission of the landlord or allow any key to be in the possession of any other person except those who are party to this agreement.

8. Permit any illegal or immoral act to take place at the property.

9. Allow anything which is or may become an annoyance or nuisance to neighbouring premises or to the landlord.

10. Carry out any trade or business in the property or use it as other than a private residence. *[A tenant working on a computer from home is fine. Holding items of stock is not as it may invalidate the insurance policy and annoy neighbours too.]*

11. Allow anything on the property that may render void any policy of insurance maintained on the property.

[If you have this clause in the agreement, you must give the tenant a copy of the insurance policy so he will know what he can and can't do!]

12. Keep any flammable item such as gas cylinders, paraffin or oil on the property.

13. Insert any rubbish, corrosive substance, cooking fat or refuse material in any sink, bath, shower or pipe.

14. Keep any bird, reptile, dog, cat or other living creature in the property without seeking the landlord's permission (such permission shall not be unreasonably withheld).

15. Erect a TV or radio aerial or satellite receiver.

16. Leave or permit to be parked anything which causes an obstruction in or to any approach road or path to the property.

17. Use a washing machine or dishwasher when not in the property. *[If it leaks, you want your tenants to be there so they can do something about it!]*

18. Use the common entrance hall for purposes other than for quiet and peaceful entry.

19. Leave any item in the common hallway.

The tenant **must**:

1. Notify the landlord promptly by phone and then in writing of any defect or disrepair in the property or to the fixtures and fittings or to smoke or carbon monoxide detectors.

2. Advise the landlord of anything that could lead to a claim being made on insurance arranged on the property. In particular, to notify the landlord if the property will be left vacant for more than fourteen

days. *[If unoccupied, you need to know so you can advise the insurance company. Where unoccupied, the premiums may increase.]*

3. Notify the landlord of any change in work, home and mobile telephone numbers. *[You need to be able to contact him!]*

4. Forward all mail addressed to the landlord or to "the owner", as soon as reasonably possible, to the landlord's home address.

5. Open and forward any mail addressed to "the occupier" that is relevant to the landlord and advise the landlord of the receipt of any notice, contact or complaint from a local authority, corporation, neighbour or any other body.

6. Whenever the property is left unattended, to lock all windows and doors properly.

7. Ensure that the common hallway areas are kept in a clean and tidy condition. Where damage to the common areas is caused by tenants or their visitors to pay to the landlord the costs of making good. *[Where the lease says that the occupiers of a group of flats must take turns to clean common areas then your tenants must do this so it should be included as a clause in the agreement.]*

8. Permit the landlord, his agent or the managing agent by appointment (but at any time in the case of emergency) to come onto the property for the purposes of carrying out and completing structural repairs, decorative improvements or to examine the state and condition of the property.

9. Permit the landlord or his agent, provided that reasonable notice has been given, within the last

forty days of the tenancy to view the property with prospective occupiers.

10. Use only the allocated refuse store bins. *[Don't forget to tell them where the communal refuse bins are kept.]*

11. Take reasonable precautions to prevent frost damage. If the property is going to be empty overnight or for more than twelve hours in cold weather, enough heating must be left on to prevent the water system freezing.

12. Keep all lights, smoke alarms, carbon monoxide detectors and bulbs in working order and replace all fuses, bulbs and fluorescent tubes when necessary.

13. Clean the refrigerator and defrost it when necessary and arrange and pay for cleaning the windows every six months.

14. Use only the allocated parking space (where applicable) for the parking of one motor car or motor bike, the vehicle to have a current road fund licence.

15. Keep any allocated gardens in a neat, tidy and well-maintained condition. *[You must give him the necessary tools to do this!]*

16. Adequately heat and ventilate the property and wipe down surfaces to stop the build-up of mould growth.

17. Take reasonable precautions to keep the premises free of infestation by vermin, rodents, fleas or ants. Where any such infestation is due to the action or inaction of the tenants, the tenants to be responsible for appropriate cleaning and fumigating costs and for the costs of removing such infestation.

18. At the end of the tenancy:

a) Remove all personal items from the property and, where necessary, make arrangements with the council to have any unwanted large items removed. Any personal items belonging to the tenant which are not removed after 14 days' written notice has been given may be sold within one month without compensation being paid and costs associated with their removal will be deducted from the deposit.

b) If the carpets have been badly soiled, arrange for and pay (at the tenant's own expense) the cost of hot water extraction steam carpet cleaning – this work to be carried out by a professional carpet cleaning company. *[Only include this clause if the property was steam cleaned at the start. For some reason, even the nicest tenants are remarkably resistant to getting this done!]*

c) Return all keys to the property to the landlord.

d) Properly clean the property.

The landlord **will**:

1. Allow the tenant to hold and enjoy the property for as long as the tenant performs his obligations under this agreement.

2. Insure the property and the items listed on the inventory, and arrange for any damage caused by an insured risk to be remedied as soon as possible.

3. Keep in good repair the structure and exterior of the property and the installations for the supply of water (including heating and hot water), electricity,

gas and sanitation and the fixtures and fittings (including mechanical and electrical items) included in the inventory.

Diplomatic immunity

The tenant cannot claim diplomatic immunity under any aspect of this Agreement.

Rent review

If the landlord agrees to extend the tenancy beyond the fixed term, the rent amount will be adjusted annually by the landlord giving at least two months' notice.

Agent

Any person other than the tenant, who pays the rent due to the landlord, shall be deemed to have made such payments as agent for and on behalf of the tenant.

Notices

The address at which the tenant may serve notices on the landlord is **INSERT YOUR ADDRESS**. *[It's a legal requirement to state your address.]*

Any notices or other documents shall be served upon the tenant by either being left at the property or being sent to the tenant at the property by first class or recorded delivery post.

Should the tenancy be extended beyond the end of the initial term, the notice period required from the tenant to end the tenancy is one month.

Data Protection

The landlord or his agent may share details about the

tenant's performance of obligations under this agreement with credit reference agencies for referencing purposes and rental decisions and with utility providers, council tax, housing benefit departments and mortgage lenders to help prevent dishonesty and for occasional debt tracing and fraud prevention.

Making rent payments
Payments are to be made to the landlord's account at **INSERT YOUR BANK NAME, BRANCH ADDRESS, SORT CODE AND THE NAME AND NUMBER OF YOUR ACCOUNT**.

Inventory
The landlord does not have facilities to store any items that the tenant does not require.

Fixtures, fittings, furnishings and effects must be left in the same place and condition at the end of the tenancy as they were at the start.

Tenants are to pay for the washing (including ironing) of all linen and for the washing and cleaning (including ironing) of all blankets and curtains which have been soiled during the tenancy.

LIST ALL ITEMS ON INVENTORY
[For each item on the inventory, the condition, make and model number should be noted and whether operating instructions have been provided. Describe the condition of carpets, curtains, walls and windows with any marks or flaws noted.

The tenant should initial, against the description of each item and for the number of keys received. It is recommended that all landlords appoint an independent inventory clerk to carry out the inventory and a schedule of condition at check-in and at move-out. This should include time-dated photos and ideally a video. It is best if the same clerk does both check-in and check-out inventories.]

I have read and understood this Agreement and have received a copy of the Energy Performance Certificate. Signature of Landlord and Tenant(s) (including Guarantors if relevant)

_____

_____

[If you use a guarantor add the following statement which should be signed by the guarantor and witnessed and signed by a third party:]

I hereby guarantee to **INSERT YOUR NAME** that in return for you granting the above tenancy to **INSERT TENANT'S NAME(S)**, I will pay rent to you in the event of failure of **INSERT TENANT'S NAME(S)** to pay it and will make good to you any losses, costs or expenses that you incur as a result of failure of **INSERT TENANT'S NAME(S)** to observe any aspect of the tenancy agreement.

Appendix 2:

USEFUL CONTACTS

Chapter 2
National Landlords Association
22-26 Albert Embankment, London, SE1 7TJ
Tel: 020 7840 8900
www.landlords.org.uk

Residential Landlords Association
1 Roebuck Lane, Sale, Manchester, M33 7SY
Tel: 0845 666 5000
www.rla.org.uk

Scottish Association of Landlords
22 Forth Street, Edinburgh, EH1 3LH
Tel: 0131 270 4774
www.scottishlandlords.com

Landlords' Association of Northern Ireland
197 Lisburn Road, Belfast, BT9 7EJ
Tel: 028 9082 7033
www.lani.org.uk

Chapter 3

The following are good websites for local information. On all these sites you can obtain information for the specific postcode you are buying into.

www.homecheck.co.uk
Offers free reports on the risk of flooding, subsidence, radon, coal mining, landslip, landfill sites, air quality and pollution.

www.upmystreet.co.uk
Gives information on house prices, council performance, school information and transport. Includes a particularly good facility where you can chart and compare historical house price performance for different postcodes.

www.hometrack.co.uk (0845 013 2350)
and www.rightmove.co.uk
Are good for information on house prices and trends.

www.houseprices.co.uk
Is a very easy site to use for recent house prices in any given area.

www.environment-
agency.gov.uk/homeandleisure/floods/31650.aspx
(0845 988 1188)
Has flood maps by postcodes.

www.hmrc.gov.uk
This is the Inland Revenue's website.

www.communities.gov.uk (020 7944 4400) has lots of useful data on a wide variety of things such as house prices, rents and regeneration initiatives.

Land Registry
www.landreg.gov.uk

Association of Residential Managing Agents (ARMA)
www.arma.org.uk (020 7978 2607)

Leasehold Advisory Service
www.lease-advice.org (020 7383 9800)

Companies House
www.companieshouse.gov.uk (0303 1234 500)

Website giving information on upcoming auctions:
www.Eigroup.co.uk

Chapter 5
Royal Institute of British Architects
www.riba.org (020 7580 5533)

Royal Institution of Chartered Surveyors
www.rics.org (0870 333 1600)

Gas Safe Register (0800 408 5500)
www.GasSafeRegister.co.uk

The Chartered Institute of Plumbing and Heating Engineering (IPHE)
www.ciphe.org.uk (01708 472 791)

The Association of Plumbing and Heating Contractors (APHC)
www.aphc.co.uk (0121 711 5030)

National Inspection Council for Electrical Installation Contracting
www.niceic.org.uk (0870 013 0382)

Electrical Contractors Association (ECA)
www.eca.co.uk (020 7313 4800)

Chapter 7
Royal Mail
www.royalmail.com (0845 774 0740)

Chapter 8
For IPHE, APHC – see Chapter 5 above. For ARMA see Chapter 3 above.

Energy Saving Trust
www.est.co.uk (0800 512 012)
England 020 7222 0101
Wales 029 2046 8340
Scotland 0131 555 7900
Northern Ireland 028 9072 6007
www.boilers.co.uk

The Energy Saving Trust's website offers useful help including a range of grants that may be available. With the site boilers.co.uk, you can type in what your specific needs are, size of home, energy source, etc, and the site will come up with suggestions starting with the most efficient model and information on grant availability.

For Land Registry – see Chapter 3 above.

Oyez Stationers
www.oyezforms.co.uk

www.landlordzone.co.uk (0845 260 4420)

www.landlordlaw.co.uk

www.LettingFocus.com

Chapter 9
For Oyez Stationers, see Chapter 8 above.

Court Service
www.hmcourts-service.gov.uk

Chapter 10
Inland Revenue
www.hmrc.gov.uk
or contact local tax office

Chapter 11
Smith & Williamson
www.smith.williamson.co.uk (020 7131 4000)

INDEX

GETTING THE BUILDERS IN
. . . and staying in control

Everyone has heard the horror stories: rogue contractors, shoddy workmanship, ballooning costs, endless delays, excuses and prevarication.

Getting the Builders In can put an end to that. It is a clear, comprehensive guide to employing a contractor. It covers conversions/ extensions, double glazing, fitted kitchens and other household projects. Here you will find expert advice on:

- Selecting contractors, and getting the right price
- Overseeing works, and knowing when to intervene
- Legal matters, including planning permission and advice on contracts

This book puts *you* firmly in the 'driving seat', improving your chances of a first-class job – without being ripped off!

Author Paul Grimaldi has worked for 30 years in construction project management. His book distils the best of his vast experience.

Three Ways to order *Right Way* books:

1. Visit www.constablerobinson.com and order through our website.
2. Telephone the TBS order line on 01206 255 800.
   Order lines are open Monday – Friday, 8:30am–5:30pm.
3. Use this order form and send a cheque made payable to TBS Ltd or
   charge my ☐ Visa ☐ Mastercard ☐ Maestro (issue no. _____)

Card number: _____

Expiry date: _____ Last three digits on back of card:_____

Signature: _____

(your signature is essential when paying by credit or debit card)

No. of copies	Title	Price	Total
	Getting the Builders In	£9.99	
	Internet Marketing	£7.99	
	Going Self-Employed	£5.99	
	For P&P add £2.75 for the first book, 60p for each additional book		
	Grand Total		£

Name: _____

Address:_____

_____ Postcode: _____

Daytime Tel. No./Email _____
(in case of query)

**Please return forms to Cash Sales/Direct Mail Dept.,
The Book Service, Colchester Road, Frating Green,
Colchester CO7 7DW.**

Enquiries to readers@constablerobinson.com.

Constable and Robinson Ltd (directly or via its agents)
may mail, email or phone you about promotions or products.

☐ Tick box if you do not want these from us ☐ or our subsidiaries.

www.constablerobinson.com/rightway